CONTENTS

Chapter One: What is Mental Illness?

Chapter Two: Seeking Help

Introduction

Mental Wellbeing is the eighty-fourth volume in the **Issues** series. The aim of this series is to offer up-to-date information about important issues in our world.

Mental Wellbeing looks at the many different types of mental illness and the types of help available.

The information comes from a wide variety of sources and includes:
Government reports and statistics
Newspaper reports and features
Magazine articles and surveys
Web site material
Literature from lobby groups
and charitable organisations.

It is hoped that, as you read about the many aspects of the issues explored in this book, you will critically evaluate the information presented. It is important that you decide whether you are being presented with facts or opinions. Does the writer give a biased or an unbiased report? If an opinion is being expressed, do you agree with the writer?

Mental Wellbeing offers a useful starting-point for those who need convenient access to information about the many issues involved. However, it is only a starting-point. At the back of the book is a list of organisations which you may want to contact for further information.

*****

Mental Wellbeing

ISSUES

Volume 84

Editor

Craig Donnellan

First published by Independence
PO Box 295
Cambridge CB1 3XP
England

British Library Cataloguing in Publication Data
Mental Wellbeing – (Issues Series)
I. Donnellan, Craig II. Series
362.2

ISBN 1 86168 279 4

Printed in Great Britain
MWL Print Group Ltd

Typeset by
Claire Boyd

Cover
The illustration on the front cover is by
Pumpkin House.

Statistics on mental health

Some quick facts

How many people in the UK have a mental health problem?

- 1 in 4 people will experience some kind of mental health problem in the course of a year.

What are the main types of mental health problems?

- 1 in 6 people will have depression at some point in their life. Depression is most common in people aged 25-44 years.
- 1 in 10 people are likely to have a 'disabling anxiety disorder' at some stage in their life. For manic depression and schizophrenia this figure is 1 in 100.

Who develops mental health problems?

- 20 per cent of women and 14 per cent of men in England have some form of mental illness.
- 18 per cent of women have a 'neurotic disorder' such as anxiety, depression, phobias and panic attacks, compared with 11 per cent of men.
- Men are three times more likely than women to have alcohol dependence and twice as likely to be dependent on drugs.

What about mental health problems among children and young people?

- 15 per cent of pre-school children will have mild mental health problems and 7 per cent will have severe mental health problems.
- 6 per cent of boys and 16 per cent of girls aged 16-19 are thought to have some form of mental health problem.

What is the prevalence of mental health problems in older people?

- 15 per cent of people over 65 have depression.
- Up to 670,000 people in the UK have some form of dementia. Five per cent of people over 65 and 10

the Mental Health Foundation

to 20 per cent of people over 80 have dementia.

What about suicide and self-harm?

- 75 per cent of all suicides are by men.
- 20 per cent of all deaths of young people are by suicide.
- 17 per cent of all suicides are by people aged 65 or over.
- Approximately 142,000 hospital admissions each year in England and Wales are the result of deliberate self-harm. Approximately 19,000 of these are young people.
- Self-harm is more common in women than in men.

What is the relationship between mental health problems and offending?

- 10-20 per cent of young people

involved in criminal activity are thought to have a 'psychiatric disorder'.
- In England and Wales an estimated 66 per cent of the remand population had mental health problems compared with 39 per cent of the sentenced population.

What are the costs of mental health problems?

- The total cost of mental health problems in England has been estimated at £32 billion. More than a third of this cost (almost £12 billion) is attributed to lost employment and productivity related to schizophrenia, depression, stress and anxiety.
- Over 91 million working days are lost to mental ill health every year. Half of the days lost through mental illness are due to anxiety and stress conditions.

- The above information is from the Mental Health Foundation's web site which can be found at www.mentalhealth.org.uk

© *Mental Health Foundation*

What are mental health problems?

Information from the Scottish Association for Mental Health (SAMH)

An illness like any other . . .

'Mental illness' is a shorthand term for a variety of illnesses that affect the functioning of the mind. It is a catch-all phrase that covers a wide range of symptoms and experiences, and like 'physical illness' it has many permutations. 'Mental illness' can refer to conditions as diverse as depression, anxiety, phobias, eating disorders and schizophrenia.

People are not born with a mental illness, nor is it part of someone's personality. It is an illness like any other, and can last anything from several weeks to a lifetime. Some people's genetic makeup may make them more susceptible to mental illness, or outside factors such as poverty, bereavement or abuse can be the cause. Like physical ailments mental illness often has a combination of causes.

Anyone can suffer from a mental illness. This includes doctors, lawyers, policemen, politicians and journalists. One in five Scots is affected by mental illness at any one time. This translates into 25 MSPs, 2 members of the Scottish Football Team or over 1000 Strathclyde Police Officers.

Mental illness is often hidden, and symptoms are not usually apparent to the outside world. Many people prefer to keep their illness a secret, for fear of stigma or discrimination in the workplace or in the street. This means that your GP, colleagues at work, friends or even family may have an illness you know nothing about.

The term 'mental illness' carries a multitude of emotive and negative connotations. So it's hardly surprising that most of us are terrified when first diagnosed. But it's important to remember that mental illness needn't be a life sentence. It may lead to a life which is a wee bit different, but it can also be a life that's fulfilling, productive, and in the main happy.

Are learning disabilities and mental illness the same sort of thing?

No. Mental illness and learning disabilities are often confused or lumped together but are quite distinct.

The term 'learning disability' was adopted by the Department of Health in 1992. It has the same meaning as its predecessor 'mental handicap', but is seen as more acceptable, particularly in reducing the confusion with mental illness. Learning disabilities start before adulthood, usually from birth and have a lasting effect on development (although everyone has the potential to stretch their capabilities with the right support).

'Mental illness' is a shorthand term for a variety of illnesses that affect the functioning of the mind

---

Learning disabilities may be mild, moderate, severe or profound, but these adjectives can only very generally suggest the level of ability. People with learning disabilities have many different talents, qualities, strengths and support needs. It is only a minority who have major difficulties in communicating their ideas and preferences.

People with learning disabilities may look or act slightly different from the norm. This makes them vulnerable to discrimination and abuse within the community. Like those of us that suffer from mental health problems, people with learning disabilities face the stigma that comes from ignorance and fear.

What the words really mean

Schizophrenia

Schizophrenia is a condition which distorts thoughts and perceptions. Sometimes the outside world feels overwhelming, and even simple decisions like what to buy in the supermarket seem impossible. You may hear voices from inside your head. These voices will seem entirely real, and impossible to distinguish from those outside. Thoughts will become jumbled and communication difficult. You may experience delusions and believe the TV is trying to control you. This can be a terrifying world to inhabit. Schizophrenia is mostly episodic – a third of people who have experienced schizophrenia only experience one episode and make a full recovery – for others less fortunate it can mean years of fluctuating between good health and illness – and some are constantly ill. Schizophrenia does not mean having a split or dual personality.

Depression

Depression is more than a fit of the blues. It is a continuous and all-consuming sense of hopelessness and despair. Severe depression will affect your sleep, your sex drive and every aspect of your life. You feel worthless and lethargic. You may struggle to stay awake and lose interest in all the things that formerly gave you pleasure. Sometimes people will get better by themselves – without intervention. Others will experience recurrent bouts of depression in-between periods of good health.

Manic depression

Manic depression is a depressive condition punctuated by episodes of extreme euphoria. It usually occurs in cycles, with long periods of depression followed by a manic high. If you are going through the manic phase of the illness you may require little or no sleep. You will be excitable, talkative, and feel full of energy, vigour and confidence. You may feel flamboyant and spend immense amounts of money without regard to the consequences. The depressive aspect of the illness usually lasts longer than the manic episodes and is characterised by all the major symptoms of depression.

People are not born with a mental illness, nor is it part of someone's personality. It is an illness like any other, and can last anything from several weeks to a lifetime

---

Obsessive compulsive conditions

Obsessive compulsive conditions are portrayed with great humour and understanding in the 1998 movie *As good as it gets*. Jack Nicholson's character feels compelled to perform

Mind your language please

Schizophrenic is possibly the most misused word in the English language. According to the press, football games, interest rates, the Government, students, Radio 1, and Middlesbrough have all been 'schizophrenic' at one time or another. And it is not just 'schizophrenic' either. Angry footballers are almost always psychotic and aggressive or violent acts are invariably 'insane', 'mad' or 'crazy'. In fact any capricious, inconsistent or paradoxical behaviour automatically assumes a mental health label. Sometimes we trivialise terms by overuse – e.g. 'I'm feeling depressed' (when we mean feeling 'down') just like we say 'I'm starving' (when we mean 'hungry').

The inappropriate use of such terms is insulting to people with mental health problems. We don't call those footballers who miss the goal, a big cancerous mole or an AIDS virus. And it's a long time since it was socially acceptable to call someone a 'mongol'. So why is it okay to use schizo, psycho, heidcase or nutter as terms of abuse?

a series of bizarre and seemingly irrational rituals to make it through the day. Compulsive hand washing and cleanliness is a common feature of obsessive compulsive conditions. You may be fully aware

that this repetitive behaviour is fruitless or ineffectual, but still be unable to stop.

Anxiety

Anxiety is something that most people experience every now and again. It is a natural reaction to stressful situations such as sitting a driving test or meeting the in-laws for the first time. You may feel tense, your mouth may dry out, you may start to shake or sweat. For some people this state of anxiety will happen every day. This is called generalised anxiety because it isn't linked to any particular stressful event. Other forms of anxiety include panic attacks and phobias.

Alcohol misuse

Alcohol misuse is not a mental illness. People can (and often do) use alcohol with no palpable effect on their quality of life. But sometimes alcohol or drug misuse is a symptom of mental illness. If you are stressed or depressed you might turn to alcohol for comfort and relief. This is sometimes known as self-medication. It's not always easy to distinguish between alcohol misuse and mental illness. Does someone drink because of a mental illness, or is their mental illness brought on by drink?

■ The above information is from the Scottish Association for Mental Health's (SAMH) web site which can be found at www.samh.org.uk

© The Scottish Association for Mental Health (SAMH)

The lowdown on mental breakdowns

Every year, one in four of us will experience a mental health problem. Some have a complete breakdown. But how do you stop it happening to you and, just as importantly, help those that have already been there?

By Kieren McCarthy

You're just as likely to be touched by mental illness as a serious physical illness, but we often find it difficult to talk about. Outside the medical profession discussion tends to be confined to what to do with 'nutters' who attack people or expression of the view that depressed people should 'snap out of it'.

The likelihood of suffering from mental illness is the same as your chances of being affected by a serious physical illness, with one in four people experiencing mental health problems every year. There is also clear evidence that discrimination against and stigmatisation of people with mental health problems is staggeringly high. Battles have been fought and won in cases of disability, race, sex and sexual preferences. Now it seems it is time to confront the prejudices surrounding mental illness.

Education, education, education

A vital part of tackling mental health is education, explains Professor Arthur Crisp, chairman of the Royal Society of Psychiatrists' 'Changing Minds' campaign.

'One way to improve the situation is to enable people to empathise, to put themselves in the place of the other person. And this is something that can be taught, especially at an early age, in schools,' he says.

That aim is the mainstay behind a government-backed campaign, 'Mind Out', which encourages famous people to talk openly about their own problems. The initiative is also targeting employers, the media and students in the hope that a more informed and balanced view of mental health will permeate through society.

'Three in ten employees will experience some kind of mental health problem in any one year,' says Mind Out. 'Employers can make a massive contribution on mental health issues – and they have a lot to gain.'

The campaign also points out that half of all press reports on mental illness link the condition with violence and criminality. Other important statistics listed by Mind Out include: a quarter of all drugs prescribed on the NHS are for mental health problems; prescriptions for antidepressants rose by more than 100 per cent between 1990 and 1995; stress-related absences account for half of all work sick-days; and one in four people with a mental illness has not consulted a professional. The list goes on and on.

Warning signs

Of course, it's not just society that needs to understand mental health better; it's also individuals – many of whom will come across their own problems at some point and may refuse to recognise the early signs.

According to a spokeswoman for the Mental Health Foundation,

early warning signs can include disturbed sleep, depression or anxiety, agitation, tiredness or lethargy, or changes in weight or appetite. But, she admits, 'It is difficult to spot and difficult to say what it will be for any particular individual.'

Prof Crisp says the very nature of different mental illnesses means that those suffering are unlikely to come to terms with their problem or seek help. 'Depression is the experience of failure, they will be losing control of feelings, low in energy, feeling worthless.

'Those with schizophrenia will definitely be protesting that they are not ill and will be unable to think clearly. Eating disorders and drug and alcohol problems are ways of coping – only when they see this is failing do they seek help.'

It's tough to talk

For those that do see people suffering, the stigma and lack of education about such disorders means people are unlikely to help. 'The public reports that they see people with certain illnesses as dangerous, others as having brought it upon themselves,' says Prof Crisp.

'But what is most clear is that people view those with mental illnesses as difficult to communicate with, and to some degree they are right.'

Prof Crisp says the combination of people who are obviously ill and induce public fear, and media that concentrate on extreme examples, means we all tend to distance ourselves from those with such problems.

With Mind Out reporting that 34 per cent of those with mental illness have been dismissed or forced to resign from their jobs, and 47 per cent saying that they have been abused or harassed in public (14 per cent physically), it's hardly surprising that the majority of sufferers choose to keep shtum.

Taking action

Perhaps what is least understood is that mental illness is remarkably similar to physical illness. Some people are genetically predisposed to it, just as some are more likely to develop cancer.

A huge number recover and re-evaluate their lives for the better, in much the same way a heart-attack patient changes their life or someone quits their job to follow their dreams if they get over a bad illness.

The prime minister's former director of communications, Alastair Campbell, recently spoke about his nervous breakdown in 1986. After he got over it he re-ordered his life, came out of it all the stronger, and went on to hold one of the most powerful posts in the country.

Prof Crisp says recovery is much like getting over a physical illness. 'Sometimes it is a short period, sometimes for ever.' He does stress however that people do need help. And this is reiterated by both Mind Out and the Mental Health Foundation.

Talking to family and friends can certainly help clarify things and self-help remedies such as taking exercise also play a part. But anyone who feels they may be developing a mental health problem should see a professional in the same way toothache leads people to the dentist or back pain persuades sufferers to consult a GP.

■ This article is for information purposes only. The material is in no way intended to replace professional medical care or attention by a qualified practitioner. The materials in this web site cannot and should not be used as a basis for diagnosis or choice of treatment.

■ The above information is the web site www.netdoctor.co.uk

Young people with mental health problems

Information from the Mental Health Foundation

Introduction

Mental health problems in children and young people are very common. For example:

■ Approximately 10% of children and young people have mental health problems that are severe enough to require professional help.

■ 8-11% of children and young people experience anxiety to such an extent that it affects their ability to get on with their everyday lives.

■ 2% of children under the age of 12 have some form of depression, compared with 5% of teenagers.

■ Suicide accounts for 20% of all deaths by young people.

Children and young people who experience mental health problems usually find the experience very distressing. Most learn to overcome their problems if they receive the right kind of help from family, friends or specialist support services.

Types of problems

The most common forms of mental health problems in children and young people are:

the Mental Health Foundation

■ emotional disorders, such as anxiety, phobias and depression

■ conduct disorders, such as stealing, defiance, fire-setting, and aggression

■ hyperkinetic disorders, such as attention deficit (hyperactivity) disorder

■ developmental disorders, such as delay in acquiring speech or bladder control

■ eating disorders, such as anorexia nervosa or bulimia nervosa

■ habit disorders, such as tics, sleeping problems, soiling

■ post-traumatic syndromes, following traumatic events

■ psycho-somatic disorders, such as chronic fatigue symptoms

■ psychotic disorders, such as schizophrenia and manic depression.

Risk factors

Some children and young people are more likely to develop mental health problems. Risk factors include:

■ genetic influences, such as a family history of mental health problems

■ low IQ and learning disability

■ other health or development problems, such as physical illness

■ communication difficulties

■ academic failure or low self-esteem

■ overt parental conflict including divorce

■ death and loss, including loss of friendship

■ abuse, neglect or bullying

■ inconsistent or unclear discipline

■ poverty, unemployment or crime.

Resilience factors

Some children and young people are less likely to develop mental health problems. Resilience factors include:

■ higher intelligence

■ easy temperament when an infant

■ secure attachments and affection from others

- positive attitude
- good communication skills
- at least one good parent-child relationship
- supervision and discipline from carers and teachers
- wider supportive network, for example caring grandparents
- school with positive policies on key issues, such as bullying
- good standard of living.

Getting help

If you are a young person in distress:

- Remember you are not alone! One in five young people will experience some kind of mental health problem in the course of a year.
- Find a friend. You may find it helpful to talk to your boyfriend or girlfriend, your best friend or a relative about your problems. If there is no one close you may prefer to talk to someone else you can trust, like a teacher, a GP or a spiritual adviser.

    If you need someone to talk to urgently and in confidence – the Samaritans are able to offer emotional support 24 hours a day on 08457 90 90 90 or visit their website at www.samaritans.org.uk
- Helplines. You may prefer to speak to someone who doesn't know you but who understands your problems and who won't judge you.
- If you have been diagnosed with a particular mental health problem, such as anxiety or depression, you may find it useful to look at our factsheets on these specific conditions.

If you are the parent or carer

- The most important thing you can do is to be there for your child and to actively listen to what they say.
- How you resolve your child's problems will depend on your personal circumstances but you are more likely to succeed if you work with your child rather than against them. Ultimately, most children have to resolve their own problems – however difficult that may be for you as an adult.
- If your child has been diagnosed with a particular mental health problem e.g. anxiety or depression, you may find it useful to look at our factsheets on these specific conditions.
- If you feel you need outside help, you may wish to contact your GP or Social Worker who can put you in touch with specialist services, such as your local Child and Adolescent Mental Health Services team.

Our work

The Mental Health Foundation undertakes a range of work with children and young people including:

- A peer support project which trains pupils to provide support and a listening ear to others.
- Training manuals to promote mental health in schools.
- Developing community mental health crisis services for young people which are specific to and responsive to their needs.
- Exploring the mental health needs of young offenders, looked-after children, homeless young people and those with emotional and behavioural difficulties.
- Examining the reasons why particular families don't engage in early intervention parenting programmes to ensure that the services understand how to keep those in most need engaged.

- The above information is from the Mental Health Foundation's web site: www.mentalhealth.org.uk

© The Mental Health Foundation

Depression

The causes, symptoms and types

Depression is a big term which covers a large range of psychological distress, from lowered moods to suicidal feelings.

More than 2.9 million Britons are thought to be suffering from some form of the condition at any one time.

Here we present a guide to the causes, symptoms and different types of the illness. If you need help with the illness you will also find the details of support groups at the end of the article.

Causes of depression

There are many causes for depression. They include:
- A family history of the illness

By Charlotte Harding, femail.co.uk

- Traumatic experiences in the past
- Stress
- Money worries
- A lack of supportive relationships.

    Often the cause is a mixture of these factors. The condition may also be linked to a series of physical causes including a poor diet, lack of physical fitness or illnesses such as flu.

    Frequent use of recreational drugs can also lead to depression because they may disrupt the brain's chemicals.

Symptoms of depression

There are many symptoms of depression. They include:
- Feelings of persistent sadness, loss of self-confidence or self-esteem, lack of enjoyment in things that used to be pleasurable or interesting
- Feelings of hopelessness and helplessness, undue feelings of guilt and worthlessness
- Feeling agitated or anxious, finding it hard to function at work or college, difficulty concentrating
- Thoughts of suicide and death.

    Other physical symptoms include tiredness, loss of energy, sleeping problems, loss of appetite or overeating, loss of sex drive or sexual problems, drinking or smoking more than normal, physical aches and pains and self-harm.

If you have experienced four or more of these symptoms for most of the day nearly every day for more than two weeks then you should seek help.

Types of depression

Reactive depression

This is thought to be the most common type of depression. It is triggered by a traumatic, difficult or stressful life event. People affected will feel low, irritable, anxious or even angry.

This can also follow a prolonged period of stress and even happen some time after the stressful period is over. Triggers vary hugely from person to person, ranging from moving house to losing a parent in childhood to a long-term disability, bereavement or divorce.

Endogenous depression

This type of depression is not always triggered by a stressful life event and is more likely to be caused by a chemical imbalance in the brain. This type of depression is often the type of depression that runs in families.

Manic depression

One in every 100 people will experience manic depression at some point in their life. This type of depression – also known as bi-polar depression – is very different from all the other types listed above. Rather than feeling unhappy all the time, the sufferer experiences big highs and excesses of energy and elation followed by big lows and feelings of utter despair. These high or low phases can last for several months at a time.

Sufferers can also some-times suffer from delusions and hallucinations – seeing things and hearing things that don't exist. Most people who suffer this type of de-pression will first experience it in their late teens to early 20s.

Like other types of depression, it is thought that a mixture of environmental and

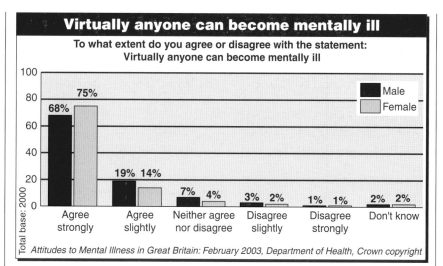

Virtually anyone can become mentally ill

To what extent do you agree or disagree with the statement:
Virtually anyone can become mentally ill

Male / Female

Agree strongly: 68% / 75%
Agree slightly: 19% / 14%
Neither agree nor disagree: 7% / 4%
Disagree slightly: 3% / 2%
Disagree strongly: 1% / 1%
Don't know: 2% / 2%

Total base: 2000

Attitudes to Mental Illness in Great Britain: February 2003, Department of Health, Crown copyright

physical factors may be to blame. Although no firm genetic link has yet been established for the illness, if you have one parent with the condition you have a ten per cent likelihood of developing the condition.

Post-natal depression

This is now a well-recognised form of depression which affects between ten and 20 per cent of women after they give birth. It should not be confused with the 'baby blues', an extremely common but short-lived period of unhappiness which occurs three or four days after giving birth. The baby blues causes crying spells and feelings of loneliness for a few days after giving birth.

Post-natal depression is a far more serious condition which starts two to three weeks after delivery and which often develops slowly so that it can be very difficult to diagnose. It can also be very difficult for the mother to recognise that she is suffering from the condition, which will compound the situation. The condition is caused by a hormonal imbalance in the brain.

Seasonal affective disorder

This type of depression, commonly known as SAD, appears with the approach of winter and is thought to be due to the lack of daylight in the winter months. This lack of daylight limits the amount of serotonin, a happy hormone in our brains, causing feelings of unhappiness.

This type of depression is often treated with light therapy.

Where to get more help

Depression Alliance provides in-formation, support and under-standing to anyone affected by depression. For a free information pack call Tel: 020 7633 0557, Fax: 020 7633 0559, E-mail information@depressionalliance.org or write to us at 35 Westminster Bridge Road, London, SE1 7JB (enclosing an SAE).

Call the Fellowship of Depressives Anonymous on 01702 433838 for support and encourage-ment for former depressives.

Call the Manic Depression Fellowship on 020 7793 2600 or visit their website on www.icmedicine.co.uk for help with manic depression.

For information on seasonal affective disorder (the winter blues) visit the SAD Association's website on www.sada.org.uk

For information on post-natal depression visit the Association For Postnatal Illness's website on www.apni.org

Mental illness in your family?

Information from the YoungMinds Booklet *Mental illness in your family?*

If someone in your family is mentally ill, this article may help you. It might be your mum or dad, brother, sister, grandparent, aunt or uncle who is not well.

A lot of people feel worried or frightened when they hear the words 'mental illness'. But this is probably because they don't understand what it means or they have heard stories which are untrue. Once you know more about mental illness, you should find it's not as frightening as you first thought.

Just as people's bodies can become unwell, people's minds can become unwell, too. Mental illness is more common than you might think.

There are different kinds of physical illness and different ways to treat them. There are also different types of mental illness and different types of treatment for them. But mental illness is something most people find hard to talk about.

This article gives you some information about mental illness, how to cope with your feelings about it, and where you can get more information and advice.

the children's
YoungMinds
mental health charity

What is mental illness?

It is important to be sure what we mean by mental illness. Most of us cope well enough with our lives on a day-to-day basis. But there are times when we don't feel so well. We get fed up, lonely, disappointed; we become anxious or frightened. We feel misunderstood and let things get out of proportion.

These kinds of feelings are part and parcel of ordinary living. But sometimes they get on top of us – so much so that we find we can't get on with our lives. We can't concentrate and sometimes we can't get to work or school. We seem to be at odds – with other people and with ourselves. Our behaviour gets 'out of order' and we become restless, argumentative, even violent. We are not happy. We don't feel well.

When our lives become as difficult as this, we have mental health problems. They can be mild or severe – some get better quickly but sometimes they last a long time and people need a lot of help.

The term 'mental illness' refers to the extreme end of these difficulties when some people, at different times of their lives, become so confused and out of touch with reality that they can barely cope with everyday living.

What are the symptoms of mental illness?

We can all see if someone has a broken leg, but it's not so easy to tell if someone is mentally ill. And because some symptoms might upset or frighten you, it can be hard to feel nice or kind to someone with a mental illness. These are some examples of mental illness:

Psychosis

Psychosis is a serious mental illness. It means that people who suffer from it (described as 'psychotic') lose touch with reality and cannot tell the difference between what is real and unreal.

The most common forms of psychotic illness are 'schizophrenia' and 'bi-polar affective disorder'.

Someone who has schizophrenia may have any of these symptoms:

- delusions, which means they believe something is real when it isn't; they may think, for example, they are famous or have special powers. They may think that they are guilty of terrible crimes or that other people are controlling their thoughts or are wanting to hurt them;
- thought disorder, which means their thoughts become very muddled and hard for anyone else to understand;
- hallucinations, which means that they see or hear or smell or feel something that isn't really there. A lot of people who have schizophrenia hear voices which no one else can hear. They might also talk back to these voices.

Having schizophrenia can make people lose interest in everyday living and make it hard for them to talk or show affection or even to eat or dress properly.

People who have bi-polar affective disorder suffer from extreme changes of mood. People who have this disorder (also called 'manic depressive illness' or 'manic depression'), can switch from being very 'manic' to being very 'depressed'. When 'manic' or 'high' they feel very happy and powerful, and may take unusual risks. When they are very 'depressed' they have little energy or enthusiasm.

People who are psychotic need help from mental health professionals.

Anxiety disorders

Some people become overwhelmed by their fears and thoughts which can lead to the development of anxiety disorders. They may have:

Phobias: severe and unreasonable fears; e. g. they are afraid of going outside, going to work or school or of being in small spaces like a lift or crowded bus, or of being in large spaces.

Obsessive compulsive disorders: they feel they have to repeat things over and over again, such as washing their hands or checking the oven is switched off, or have thoughts they can't get out of their mind.

. . . because some symptoms might upset or frighten you, it can be hard to feel nice or kind to someone with a mental illness

---

Eating disorders: they feel so worried about the shape of their bodies and frightened of losing control of their lives that they eat too little (anorexia nervosa) or repeatedly binge and vomit (bulimia nervosa) – which badly affects their physical growth and health.

Post-traumatic stress disorders: they feel overwhelmed by very frightening events or experiences that have happened to them, such as accidents and assaults. They may suffer flashbacks where they seem to re-live the frightening event. They often become very moody and find it hard to concentrate or sleep at night.

Clinical depression

Clinical depression is very different from just feeling low and that things are too much. People who have clinical depression feel very miserable or hopeless, sometimes for weeks or months on end. They may feel they want to kill themselves. They feel tired all the time and find it hard to concentrate. They often don't feel up to doing normal things like getting dressed or making something to eat.

Sometimes mothers get depressed after a baby is born. This is called 'post-natal depression' or, if severe, 'puerperal psychosis'. This can make doing ordinary things very hard, for example, looking after the baby or other children.

If one of your parents has a mental illness, there might be times when they can't give you the love and care you need

---

What causes mental illness?

No one really knows all the reasons why people become mentally ill. Some people have a 'chemical imbalance' which affects how their brain works. This makes them have strange thoughts or feelings, or behave oddly. They may need to take medication to help their brain work better. For other people, something might happen in their life which is very stressful, such as the death of someone very close, and this may trigger a mental illness. Mental illness doesn't normally start out of the blue. It usually develops slowly. But some people do get a mental illness suddenly, such as when someone has a psychotic illness.

How long does a mental illness last?

There is not an easy answer to this question, because it varies from one person to another.

Some people may only ever have one bout of mental illness, which lasts for a few weeks or months. Someone else may have a mental illness all their life, but learn how to live with it with support from friends or through counselling or psychotherapy. Taking medication regularly helps some people to lead a fairly normal life. Some people may have many periods of mental illness during their life, but also long periods when they are well. A few people will have to spend periods in hospital from time to time.

How does mental illness in your family affect you?

The closer the person is to you, the more likely you will find things difficult. If one of your parents has a mental illness, there might be times when they can't give you the love and care you need. They might also find it hard to do things like cook your meals or do the washing or help you with your homework.

If your brother or sister is ill, there might be times when they don't want to be with you or when they don't behave like a 'normal' brother or sister. Your parents might be very busy looking after them and sometimes you might feel your parents don't have any time for you.

Sometimes people can behave in ways which are hard to cope with and which will upset you. This can be very frightening. You might be worried that you will get hurt if someone is being aggressive. Or you might be worried they will hurt themselves.

Living with someone in your family who has a mental illness might lead you to have some uncomfortable feelings. You might also feel things you don't want to feel. It might feel unfair that you are expected to do things that other people your age don't have to do, like looking after the person who is unwell, doing lots of jobs around the house, or looking after your younger brothers or sisters. You might find you feel ashamed, or that you can't talk openly to your friends about your relative's illness. Or you might feel you don't want to bring your friends home.

You may be worried about whether the illness will ever go away or even that you are to blame in some way.

You might even be afraid that you will suffer from the same illness at some time in your life. But remember, even though some mental illnesses are more common in some families, it's much more likely that you will NOT develop a mental illness yourself. And even if you do, there will always be people who can help you.

It is normal to have any of these feelings. You are probably feeling this way because you're having to cope with something which is very hard

---

You may find it helps if you talk to someone. This might be a friend, or a youth worker, counsellor or mental health professional

---

to deal with. You may find it helps if you talk to someone. You might want to try and talk to someone else in your family, because they are having to live with the same problems as you and will know what you're going through.

Or you might want to try and think of someone else whom you like and trust. This might be a friend, or a youth worker, teacher, school nurse, counsellor, doctor, or mental health professional.

What help is there for people with mental illness?

People who have a mental illness need help from a specialist mental health service (that includes psychiatrists, psychologists, psychotherapists, social workers and nurses who are all highly trained in treating mental illness). Their GP will usually arrange this. They will be offered treatment to help them recover, or at least to help them cope better. Treatment usually starts by assessing the person's problems. Most people who have a mental illness are offered either a 'talking' treatment, such as counselling or psychotherapy, or

---

medication to help them get better. Often, they are offered both.

Sometimes, people become so ill that they need to go into hospital. Most people are willing to go because they know they need help. But sometimes, if people are very unwell, they might not realise that they need to go to hospital. Yet they might be at risk of hurting themselves or someone else, or they might need urgent treatment which can only be given in hospital. So the law says people can be taken into hospital even if they don't want to go, but only when it's in their own interest. This doesn't happen very often. The Mental Health Act states how and when this can happen.

If it is your parent or carer who is ill, social services might be able to arrange for some extra help at home. Or they might try to make sure that a close friend or relative can give your family the help it needs. Occasionally, social services will arrange for children to stay with a foster carer until their parent or carer is able to look after them again.

■ The above information is from YoungMinds, 102-108 Clerkenwell Road, London EC1M 5SA. Tel: 020 7336 8445, Parents' Information Service: 0800 018 2138; E-mail: enquiries@youngminds.org.uk, Web site: www.youngminds.org.uk

To obtain further copies of this and the other booklets in the series, contact YoungMinds. This booklet (ref B04) was published in 2003.

Alzheimer's disease

Information from the Alzheimer's Society

What is Alzheimer's disease?

Alzheimer's disease is the most common form of dementia, affecting around 500,000 people in the UK. This article outlines the symptoms and causes of Alzheimer's disease, and describes what treatments are currently available.

Alzheimer's disease, first described by the German neurologist Alois Alzheimer, is a physical disease affecting the brain. During the course of the disease 'plaques' and 'tangles' develop in the structure of the brain, leading to the death of brain cells.

We also know that people with Alzheimer's have a shortage of some important chemicals in their brain. These chemicals are involved with the transmission of messages within the brain. Alzheimer's is a progressive disease, which means that gradually, over time, more parts of the brain are damaged. As this happens, the symptoms become more severe.

Symptoms

People in the early stages of Alzheimer's disease may experience lapses of memory and have problems finding the right words. As the disease progresses they may:

- Become confused, and frequently forget the names of people, places, appointments and recent events.
- Experience mood swings. They may feel sad or angry. They may feel scared and frustrated by their increasing memory loss.
- Become more withdrawn due either to a loss of confidence or to communication problems.

As the disease progresses, people with Alzheimer's will need more support from those who care for them. Eventually they will need help with all their daily activities.

While there are some common symptoms of Alzheimer's disease, it is important to remember that everyone is unique. No two cases of Alzheimer's are likely to be the same. People always experience illness in their own individual way.

Alzheimer's
Dementia care & research

What causes Alzheimer's disease?

So far, no one single factor has been identified as a cause for Alzheimer's disease. It is likely that a combination of factors, including age, genetic inheritance, environmental factors, diet and overall general health, are responsible.

Age

Age is the greatest risk factor for dementia. Dementia affects one in 20 people over the age of 65 and one in five over the age of 80. However, Alzheimer's is not restricted to elderly people: there are over 18,000 people under the age of 65 with dementia in the UK.

Genetic inheritance

Many people fear that they may inherit Alzheimer's disease. Scientists are currently investigating the genetic background to Alzheimer's.

We do know that there are a few families where there is a very clear inheritance of the disease from one generation to the next. This is often in families where the disease appears relatively early in life.

In the vast majority of cases, however, the effect of inheritance seems to be small. If a parent or other relative has Alzheimer's disease, your own chances of developing the disease are only a little higher than if there were no cases of Alzheimer's in the immediate family.

Environmental factors

The environmental factors that may contribute to the onset of Alzheimer's disease have yet to be identified. A few years ago, there were concerns that exposure to aluminium might cause Alzheimer's disease. However, these fears have largely been discounted.

Other factors

Because of the difference in their chromosomal make-up, people with Down's syndrome who live into their 50s and 60s may develop Alzheimer's disease.

People who have had severe head or whiplash injuries appear to be at increased risk of developing dementia. Boxers who receive continual blows to the head are also at risk.

Research has also shown that people who smoke and those who have high blood pressure or high cholesterol levels increase their risk of developing Alzheimer's.

Getting a diagnosis

If you are concerned about your own health, or the health of someone close to you, it is important to seek help from a GP. An early diagnosis will:

- Help you plan for the future
- Enable the person with dementia to benefit from the treatments that are now available
- Help you identify sources of advice and support.

There is no straightforward test for dementia. A diagnosis is usually made by excluding other causes. The GP or specialist will need to rule out infection, vitamin deficiency, thyroid problems, brain tumours, the side-effects of drugs and depression.

Specialists

Your GP may ask a specialist for help in carrying out a diagnosis. The specialist may be an old-age psychiatrist, a neurologist, a physician in geriatric medicine or a general psychiatrist. Who you see depends on the age of the person being examined, how physically able they are, and how well services are developed in the area.

Tests

The person being tested will usually be given a blood test and a full physical examination to rule out or identify any other medical problems. The person's memory will be assessed, initially with questions about recent events and past memories. Their memory and thinking skills may also be assessed in detail by a psychologist.

A brain scan may be carried out to give some clues about the changes taking place in the person's brain. There are a number of different types of scan, including CT (computerised tomography) and MRI (magnetic resonance imaging).

Treatment

There is currently no cure for Alzheimer's disease. However, there are a number of drug treatments available that can ameliorate the symptoms or slow down the disease progression in some people.

People with Alzheimer's have been shown to have a shortage of the chemical acetylcholine in their brains. The drugs Aricept, Exelon

---

Much can be done at a practical level to ensure that people with Alzheimer's live as independently as possible for as long as possible

---

and Reminyl work by maintaining existing supplies of acetylcholine. These drugs are only helpful for people with mild to moderate dementia. Side-effects may include diarrhoea, nausea, insomnia, fatigue and loss of appetite.

A drug called Ebixa was launched in the UK in 2002. This drug works in a different way to the other three – it prevents the excess entry of calcium ions into brain cells. Excess calcium in the brain cells damages them and prevents them from receiving messages from other brain cells. Ebixa is the only drug

that is suitable for use in people in the middle to later stages of dementia. Side-effects may include hallucinations, confusion, dizziness, headaches and tiredness.

These drugs are not a cure, but they may stabilise some of the symptoms of Alzheimer's disease for a limited period of time.

Caring for someone with dementia

Much can be done at a practical level to ensure that people with Alzheimer's live as independently as possible for as long as possible.

The Alzheimer's Society has a range of information sheets and guides for people with dementia and their carers. Local branches also provide support to carers and people with dementia.

■ The above information is from the Alzheimer's Society's web site: www.alzheimers.org.uk

© *Alzheimer's Society*

About dementia

Information from Alzheimer's Disease International (ADI)

What is dementia?
Dementia is a term used to describe various different brain disorders that have in common a loss of thinking function. Most causes of dementia are progressive. How fast dementia progresses depends on the individual.

How many people in the world have dementia?
There are an estimated 18 million people in the world with dementia. 12 million of them live in developing countries.

Will the number of people with dementia increase in the future?
Alzheimer's Disease International believes that by 2025, the number of people with dementia will increase dramatically to 34 million.

What are the most common causes of dementia?
There are over 100 diseases that cause dementia. The most common are:
■ Alzheimer's disease accounts for

50-60% of all cases and is caused by abnormal brain tissue changes.
■ Vascular dementia is the second most common cause and refers to all forms of dementia caused by damage to blood supply to the brain.
■ Dementia with Lewy bodies is associated with abnormal collections of proteins in the brain's nerve cells.
■ Fronto-temporal dementia (such as Pick's disease) is associated with changes in the frontal lobe of the brain.

What are the early symptoms of dementia?
Every person is unique and dementia affects people differently. However, the 10 most common early symptoms of dementia include:
1. Memory loss
2. Difficulty in performing familiar tasks
3. Problems with language
4. Disorientation to time and place

5. Poor or decreased judgement
6. Problems with keeping track of things
7. Misplacing things
8. Changes in mood or behaviour
9. Changes in personality
10. Loss of initiative

Who gets dementia?
Dementia is not a normal part of ageing. Age is an important risk factor but not the only one. Dementia affects one person in 20 over the age of 65 and one person in five over the age of 80.

Prevalence rates are:

Age (years)	Prevalence
Below 64	1 in 1000
66-79	1 in 20
80-84	1 in 5
85+	1 in 3

■ The above information is from Alzheimer's Disease International's (ADI) web site which can be found at www.alz.co.uk
© *Alzheimer's Disease International (ADI)*

A beginner's article about schizophrenia

Information from the Schizophrenia Association of Great Britain (SAGB)

Self-help in recognising symptoms in yourself or others

Why should young people be interested in schizophrenia?

This article is about a disease, schizophrenia, which affects the delicate working of the brain and its neurotransmitters. As a result of the brain not working properly the behaviour, emotions and thinking of the person getting ill alter. The personality alters through disease.

A friend or relation is becoming ill

It is very difficult for others who are well to understand altered behaviour and thought in someone they have known for years. Why, they think, are they being horrible to me? Why are they so irritable? Even angry? – over nothing. Why are they so suspicious? Why do they look so ill?

You yourself are becoming ill

It really is horrible to become mentally ill. If the chemicals in your brain are not functioning properly it is very difficult not to be over-whelmed by pathological (the product of disease) thoughts coming into your head.

You may become especially suspicious (paranoid) about your best friends and think they are trying to harm you. You may find it very difficult indeed to concentrate on what your tutor or workmates are saying and, as for remembering anything, it is quite a nightmare.

You may get into trouble with the teacher because your work has suddenly become so poor when previously you had always had good marks in tests. What is happening to you? You feel the whole world is against you and you just do not know why. You feel angry because no one seems nice to you any more. Just let anyone tell you that you are bad tempered and you'll knock them for six. And what is that awful voice in your head telling you to do this and that in a most unpleasant way? How dictatorial it is! The voice seems to be real and yet no one else is there.

Psychiatric symptoms of mental illness

Just what is happening? The psych-iatric symptoms by which schizo-phrenia is diagnosed are delusions or false beliefs, hallucinations and thought disorder. The delusions may be paranoid or persecutory and the person becoming ill may believe everyone is against them when this is far from the truth, or may have thoughts that they are very powerful, grandiose and important.

Hallucinations are very difficult to explain to anyone. People may see things which are not there (visual hallucinations), or hear voices when no one else is there (auditory hallucinations). These voices are really the patient's thoughts, somehow magnified, so that they seem to be speaking out loud. The thoughts may often be of a very unpleasant nature, telling the patient to do all sorts of things quite against his or her nature.

Thought disorder is self-explanatory. Thought may become jumbled and so may speech. Some-times the mind may become a total blank, with no thoughts whatsoever. To a person becoming mentally ill

these are fearful and frightening changes in personality. If you can put yourself in such a person's shoes you can begin to feel a lot of compassion and sympathy for them. You must learn not to take offence at things said by someone becoming mentally ill. In this way, by not reacting adversely, you can become a stabilising effect on the ill person. 'Judge Not' is a very important precept.

Importance of recognising symptoms

At first, when a person is becoming mentally ill, he may not be abnormal at all for much of the time.

Unhappily his well friends will remember how horrid he has been to them when he was showing symptoms. They may feel resentment if they have not learned about mental illness. It is possible that the ill person, when feeling well, will scarcely remember his behaviour. To him it may be as a dream. It is important to remember this. Schizophrenia is a disease which often attacks the adolescent or young adult, with boys having an earlier onset usually than girls and also, very often, a more severe illness, but the illness can start at any age from childhood to old age. It is really important for everyone to be able to recognise the symptoms.

If you were so unfortunate as to be developing such an illness, a recognition of the symptoms depends, at least in part, on your having learned these symptoms. If they are firmly in your mind you might remember them and if you become ill, you can get treatment as soon as possible.

The nature of the illness

Schizophrenia is most probably not one illness but an umbrella term covering a number of different diseases, each having its own cause, but sharing the same psychiatric symptoms.

There is a genetic component (i.e. there is a hereditary aspect) to at least some of these diseases. The causes may be anywhere in the body or brain. Mostly they may start in the body and only gradually and intermittently affect the brain. On the other hand diseases of the brain, like a brain tumour or an infection like meningitis, can also upset the working of the brain.

It seems likely, from a great deal of evidence, that the origin of much psychiatric disease arises in the body. Many bodily diseases are known to give rise to psychiatric symptoms which, if untreated, can have profound effects on the brain. An American physician, the late Dr F. Curtis Dohan, produced evidence supporting his hypothesis that the eating of grains and sometimes the drinking of milk, over a long period, in someone who was genetically vulnerable to schizophrenia, eventually produced the psychiatric symptoms. Dohan thought schizophrenia was closely related to a disease of known sensitivity to grains – coeliac disease. Dohan said that, in schizophrenia, wheat, rye, oats, barley, sorghum and millet in descending order of toxicity could eventually cause psychiatric symptoms. There may often be blood sugar problems in schizophrenia which affect the glucose supply to the brain.

Infections also may be particularly severe, particularly viral infections, such as influenza, measles and glandular fever, and these infections bring on schizophrenia in someone genetically vulnerable.

The hopeful aspect of all these other diseases, which may be the cause of the psychiatric symptoms, is that, for the most part, if looked for and found, they are treatable. In these cases schizophrenia can be a curable disease.

Alcohol and street drugs

Alcohol and street drugs are very bad for those with incipient schizophrenia. They can worsen the illness and confuse the diagnosis. It is totally essential for the well-being of future generations that the present generation shuns both alcohol and street drugs. They are extraordinarily harmful to all and destructive of happiness to those who take them.

To those becoming mentally ill they are especially harmful. At first they may seem to reduce the alarming symptoms but this is only a temporary and false brightening. If you are mentally well you want to stay that way. If you are mentally ill, or potentially so, run a mile away from such temptations as alcohol and drugs.

Smoking

Many people with schizophrenia are exceedingly heavy smokers and their addiction makes them feel better for a very short period of time.

It is much better not to smoke, as smoking rapidly becomes an addiction in those becoming mentally ill and can lead to severe circulatory problems.

Food

We all need to feed our brains to derive the best we can from them. Fresh fruit and vegetables, especially raw or lightly cooked, are nourishing. Fish is an excellent food, especially fatty fish, like salmon and mackerel, but all fish is good unless you are allergic to it. If you can eat a tin of sardines a day you will get sufficient

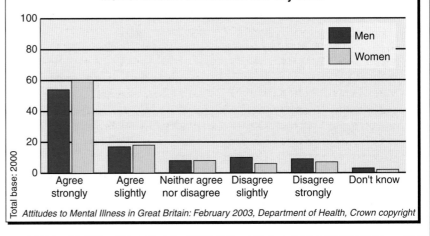

Mental illness is an illness like any other

To what extent do you agree or disagree with the statement: Mental illness is an illness like any other

Total base: 2000

Attitudes to Mental Illness in Great Britain: February 2003, Department of Health, Crown copyright

essential fatty acids which are thought to be important for people suffering from schizophrenia. Rapeseed oil, linseed oil and walnuts contain chemicals which are converted in the body to essential fatty acids. Alternatively, fish oil capsules can be taken.

Turkey, chicken and other birds are also excellent foods. It may be that for those who come from mentally unstable families a reduction in the consumption of wheat, milk and sugar is helpful. Glucose and fructose (fruit sugar) may be better sugars to take.

Symptoms to look out for. What should we do?

We know very little really about schizophrenia but try to remember the symptoms to help your friends or yourself if you find yourself losing mental stability. The sooner treatment starts, the better the response to it and the less likely the disease is to become severe.

Remember too that usually, perhaps always, there are physical symptoms that may occur before the development of the psychiatric symptoms. The patient-to-be may lose a great deal of weight. Their face may be thin and very pale. The pupils in their eyes may be large or very tiny. The patient may have digestive problems, constipation or vomiting. Some may become anorexic, particularly perhaps young women.

A flu-like condition may develop, with a slight rise in temperature. There may be a great lack of energy in the day and overactivity at night. There may be palpitations of the heart, and panic accompanying them. Such panic is overwhelming and produces great fear. Anger and violence may accompany the fear. This is quite out of the control of the patient. All our emotions are chemically caused. For the most part we are the product of our biochemical make-up. We cannot choose whether we are nice or nasty, good-tempered or bad-tempered. We can learn, though, how to restore our personality to what it was before becoming mentally ill.

Medical illnesses which could be the cause of the mental symptoms must be very thoroughly looked for

by the doctors and, if found, treated. Apparently vascular disease, gut disease, diabetes, and other endocrine (hormonal) diseases are particularly common. One American writer, Shiffler, said, 'There are no psychiatric patients, only medical patients with varying degrees of psychopathology' (psychiatric medical symptoms).

Although ideally you should be able to absorb all the necessary vitamins and minerals from your food, you may have poor gastrointestinal absorption and it could be particularly important for you to supplement your diet with extra nutrients.

Information regarding nutritional supplements can be obtained from the Schizophrenia Association of Great Britain including details of the most important fish oils. We have been greatly encouraged to find that many members report an improvement in their symptoms after taking them. The packs contain vitamins, minerals and fish oil. We do stock the nutrients and sell them at cost price to SAGB members. We can also consider requests for help with the purchase price for those who cannot afford to buy them (for as long as our own funding allows us to do this). We do not advise people to give up any medication they are on when they start taking additional nutrients.

Specific information regarding nutritional supplements can be obtained from the Schizophrenia Association of Great Britain,

including details of the most important fish oils. These supplements are available from the Association.

Summary

This is but a brief report of the sort of disease schizophrenia is. Our umbrella logo signifies not one disease but many sheltering under the name. Remember, in many of its manifestations it can be curable or, if not curable, treatable with minimal doses of medication and diet, if appropriate, and increased vitamins and minerals as described in the SAGB's Management Notes.

Do not take it out on your family and friends. Do all that you can to get well. Do not despair, and help one another, accepting always the physical basis of personality which is true for all of us and bear in mind that personality can change very slowly, often because of the onset of disease affecting the brain. You are not bad if your behaviour alters through disease, but ill.

What do I do if I feel worried about something or I need explanation, advice or help?
Do not put off doing something. Go to see your doctor or talk to your student welfare officer, personal tutor, or family.

■ The above information is from the Schizophrenia Association of Great Britain's (SAGB) web site which can be found at www.sagb.co.uk

© *Schizophrenia Association of Great Britain (SAGB)*

Anxiety disorders

The National Phobics Society guide to Anxiety Disorders

Well-known anxiety disorders

Simple or specific phobias

A phobia is an irrational fear of an object/situation etc. that would not normally trouble most people. As the name suggests, simple/specific phobias are phobias that are about specific objects, situations etc. They can be quite distinct in nature and easily identified. For example, fear of spiders, fear of thunderstorms, fear of heights. Any phobia may produce a state of panic when the sufferer is confronted with the phobic object/situation. A wide variety of physical symptoms are experienced such as nausea, increased heartbeat and jelly legs. For this reason, many people with simple or specific phobias enter into a pattern of avoidance which can vary enormously in severity from someone who would not want to touch a spider, to someone who cannot even look at a picture of a spider in magazines, and therefore has to vet everything they come into contact with. The latter demonstrates just how debilitating even a simple phobia can be.

Agoraphobia

Agoraphobia is a very complex phobia usually manifesting itself as a collection of interlinked phobias. For example many agoraphobics also fear being left alone (monophobia), dislike being in any situation where they feel trapped (exhibiting claustrophobia type tendencies) and fear travelling away from their 'safe' place, usually the home. Some agoraphobics find they can travel more easily if they have a trusted friend or family member accompanying them; however, this can quickly lead to dependency on their carer. The severity of agoraphobia varies enormously between sufferers from those who are housebound, even room-bound, to those who can travel specific distances within a defined boundary.

Social phobia

Social or public situations of any kind may induce this disorder which

national phobics society

The Anxiety Disorders Charity

is often expressed as a fear of being the centre of attention, or of others noticing the sufferer's anxious behaviour. Social phobia can also be classed as 'specific social phobia' i.e. when there is social phobia only in specific social situations, e.g. public speaking. The fear of behaving in an embarrassing or humiliating way can lead to a complete withdrawal from social contact, as well as avoidance of specific social situations such as public toilets, eating out etc. The physical manifestations of this phobia include blushing, shaking and sweating etc.

Generalised anxiety disorder (GAD)

This can be defined as a disorder in which the sufferer feels in a constant state of high anxiety. The anxiety experienced is not as a result of any specific trigger, but those with this condition feel that they are on edge all the time for no specific reason. GAD is often accompanied by depression. GAD is sometimes called 'free-floating' anxiety condition.

Panic disorder

The common thread between most anxiety disorders is the panic attack. However, when panic attacks are experienced out of the blue without an apparent trigger, this is classified as panic disorder. Sufferers of panic disorder often feel fine one minute, and yet the next may feel totally out of control and in the grips of a panic attack. Panic attacks produce very real physical symptoms from a rapid increase in heartbeat to a churning stomach sensation. These physical symptoms are naturally unpleasant and the accompanying psychological thoughts of terror can make a panic attack a very scary experience. For this reason, sufferers start to dread the next attack, and quickly enter into a cycle of living 'in fear of fear'.

Obsessive compulsive disorder (OCD)

This disorder can be looked at in two parts: obsessions – these are repetitive, obtrusive, unwanted thoughts that are experienced and result in unreasonable fears; and compulsions – acts or rituals carried out in response to fears generated by obsessions. The classic OCD condition is that of compulsive hand washing in response to an irrational fear of germs/contamination. Sufferers of this disorder feel less anxious once they

Neurotic disorders		
Prevalence of neurotic disorders among adults:[1] by sex, 2000		
Great Britain	Females	Males
Panic disorder	0.7%	0.7%
All phobias	2.2%	1.3%
Obsessive compulsive disorder	1.3%	0.9%
Depressive episode	2.8%	2.3%
Generalised anxiety disorder	4.6%	4.3%
Mixed anxiety and depressive disorder	10.8%	6.8%
Any neurotic disorder[2]	19.4%	13.5%

1 Those aged 16 to 74 years living in private households in Great Britain.
2 People may have more than one type of neurotic disorder so the percentage with any disorder is not the sum of those with specific disorders.

Source: Psychiatric Morbidity Survey, Office for National Statistics, September 2000, Crown copyright

have carried out a compulsion. It is possible to experience obsessive thoughts only and not have the desire to carry out a compulsion. Examples of compulsions are excessive cleaning, counting, checking, measuring, and repeating tasks or actions. Trichotillomania (compulsive hair-pulling) may also be classified under the general umbrella of OCD. Examples of obsessions are worrying excessively about death, germs, illness – usually AIDS, cancer, etc. (this can also be classified as an 'Illness phobia') – having undesirable sexual thoughts, fearing causing harm to others.

Body dysmorphic disorder (BDD)/ Dysmorphophobia

This disorder has also been nick-named 'Imagined Ugliness Syndrome' for sufferers of the condition have an irrational preoccupation with a perceived body defect, either present in themselves or in others; the latter being dysmorphophobia by proxy. BDD sufferers cannot accept that their fears of their perceived body defect are out of all proportion, and frequently seek plastic surgery/other measures in an attempt to rectify the perceived problem.

Post traumatic stress disorder (PTSD)

PTSD is an anxiety disorder which may develop following exposure to any one of a variety of traumatic events that involve actual or threatened death, or serious injury. The event may be witnessed rather than directly experienced, and even learning about it may be sufficient if the persons involved are family members or close friends. Sufferers may experience flashbacks, panic attacks and heightened awareness.

Trichotillomania

The main feature of trichotillomania is the recurrent pulling out of the individual's own hair which results in noticeable hair loss. Having pulled out hair from any area of the body, the tension and anxiety that sufferers of trichotillomania experience is relieved.

■ The above information is from National Phobics Society's web site which can be found at www.phobics-society.org.uk

© National Phobics Society

Other anxiety conditions/disorders/phobias

Emetophobia – (vomit phobia)
Emetophobia is a term used to describe the fear of vomiting/being sick, and is also used to describe those who fear seeing others being sick. Emetophobes often fear being sick in public, being near people who are ill with tummy bugs etc., eating out or eating food known to carry a higher than average risk of food poisoning.

Monophobia – (fear of being alone)
Monophobics typically fear being left alone as they worry about having a panic attack and having to cope alone without their 'support' person. This phobia is often associated with agoraphobia and panic disorder.

Choking phobia, Globus Hystericus & Swallowing phobia
These phobias result from anxiety which results in tension affecting the throat area. Sufferers have difficulties in swallowing, and often describe themselves as 'having a lump in the throat'.

Depersonalisation disorder (DD)
Depersonalisation is the experience of feeling unreal, detached, and often, unable to feel emotion. It is a phenomenon characterised by a disruption in self-awareness and emotional numbness. Many people experience depersonalisation during a panic attack and this is often characterised as the peak level of anxiety.

Claustrophobia – (fear of confined spaces/being trapped)
This is the fear of confined spaces/being shut in an enclosed space. Sufferers of this phobia fear that they will experience a terrifying panic attack if ever they are placed in a situation where they feel enclosed/confined.

Seasonal affective disorder (SAD)
This condition is also known as the 'Winter Blues' because those who suffer with it feel down, depressed, experience loss of energy, changes in appetite/ sleep patterns during the winter months. The condition is believed to be due to the lower light levels that are around during winter.

Toilet phobia
This term is used to describe a wide variety of fears associated with toilets, urination and defecation. Sufferers may: be unable to urinate/defecate; fear that they may soil/wet themselves and consequently worry about being too far from a toilet; fear using public toilets because of anxieties around the cleanliness of toilets, or fear that others may be scrutinising them whilst urinating (especially common amongst men).

Injection phobia – (Trypanophobia)
Trypanophobic sufferers feel panic, revulsion and symptoms of anxiety at the thought of an injection, let alone the sight of a syringe and needle. Sufferers may pass out during the course of having an injection because of intense anxiety.

Sexual phobias
Sexual phobias are often very complex phobias covering many different aspects of sexual relationships. Types of sexual phobia may include:
■ Fear of losing control of yourself and bodily functions
■ Fear of being inadequate
■ Fear of infection
■ Fear of becoming pregnant
■ Fear of intimacy
■ Fear of having abnormal genitals

Erythrophobia – (blushing phobia)
Sufferers find that their blushing is not controllable, and is often severe enough to apparently be noticed by others. The attention that sufferers receive as a consequence of blushing creates more nervousness, and in turn more blushing. This particular phobia is associated with social phobia.

Mental illness and violence

Mental health patients more likely to suffer violence

People with severe mental illness living in the community are more than twice as likely to be victims of violence as the general public, according to psychiatrists.

Since large mental hospitals closed, fears have been raised that people with severe mental illness could pose a risk to the rest of the community.

But a study of patients with psychotic disorders, including schizophrenia and manic depression, found that 16% had been victims of violence in the last year.

This compares with 6.7% of the general population in London and 7.1% in all inner cities who annually are victims of 'contact crime', according to official figures.

The survey of 708 patients with psychotic disorders who live in four inner city areas was presented on January 30, 2003 at the annual meeting of the Royal College of Psychiatry's faculty of forensic psychiatry.

Lead researcher Dr Elizabeth Walsh, a senior lecturer at the Institute of Psychiatry in London, said: 'We are always reading in the media about how people with severe mental illness are dangerous but a very small proportion of people with mental illness are dangerous.

'We might see them as a risk to us but we are probably a greater risk to them,' she said.

When the patients were asked if they had been assaulted, beaten, molested or subjected to any other form of violence in the last year, 16% answered yes.

> **'Mentally ill people need protection from society rather than society needing protection from them'**

Dr Walsh explained that people who develop psychotic illnesses tend to drop down the social scale and have problems forming relationships or keeping a job.

This meant they were more likely to end up in dangerous environments, which along with drug use and paranoia could increase the risk of being a victim of violence.

The study found that victimised patients were significantly more likely to report severe psychological symptoms, homelessness, substance misuse and previous violent behaviour.

They were twice as likely to be using an illegal drug as non-victims and four times more likely to be using two or more illegal drugs.

Some 14% of those studied admitted assaulting another person in the previous year.

Marjorie Wallace, the chief executive of mental health charity Sane, said the violence suffered by people with mental illness was a direct consequence of the failure and underfunding of care in the community.

She said: '[This] has led to mentally ill people being placed in sub-standard flats and bedsits in the most dangerous areas of towns where they are sitting ducks for drug addicts, dealers and other criminals.

'Mentally ill people need protection from society rather than society needing protection from them.'

© *Guardian Newspapers Limited 2003*

Mental illness – dispelling the stigma

Information from Everywoman

One in four people will experience some kind of mental health problem in the course of a year. It could be you or me, our friends, partners and families. However, many people with mental health problems say one of the worst aspects of their illness is the discrimination they face on a daily basis. Mind out for Mental Health is a Department of Health campaign which tackles the stigma surrounding mental health.

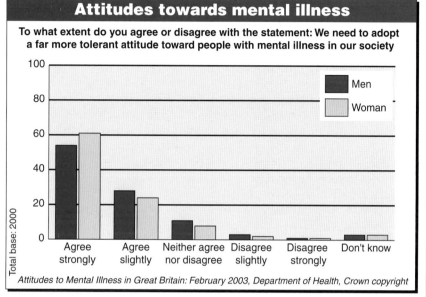

Attitudes to Mental Illness in Great Britain: February 2003, Department of Health, Crown copyright

Marjorie's story

Marjorie Thompson, 45, is a cause related marketing director who has a diagnosis of severe recurrent unipolar depression. Despite her illness, she has been the Chair of CND, worked as a cause related marketing director for a major advertising agency and co-written a best-selling book.

'Depression is the last stigma. We're not allowed to mock blacks, gays or women any more but everyone is prepared to ridicule the mentally ill – to refer to them as nutters, psychos or dangerous weirdos. People who haven't suffered from some kind of mental illness shouldn't be so smug, so sure that it will never touch their lives. There are many forms of the illness – Seasonal Affective Disorder, midlife crisis, and post-natal depression – that it's likely to hit you or someone you know at some point. It's the cancer of the 21st century. Yet the longer it remains a taboo, the longer women will go home and cry every night and men will soldier on until they kill themselves.

'A couple of years ago, I fractured my leg and was in a wheelchair for seven months. But if I had to choose now, I would rather fall down the stairs and destroy my legs than have another nervous breakdown. My mother was a life-long sufferer of manic depression and I had my first bout of depression when I was 21. The symptoms are impossible to deal with, I can't sleep, can't eat, can't concentrate.

'At 35, I had a major breakdown. I knew I wasn't mad but prayed that someone would inject me with a killer drug and put me out of my misery. Cleaning my teeth was like climbing Everest. No one ever explained depression to me, they just put me on more drugs – one of which listed death as a side effect.

'Depression is the last stigma. We're not allowed to mock blacks, gays or women any more but everyone is prepared to ridicule the mentally ill – to refer to them as nutters, psychos or dangerous weirdos'

'I was angry with myself for being "weak" and felt I might have achieved more if I had known what was happening to me earlier. I spent six months on six different kinds of drugs. I was called a loony, which is so unfair and hurtful. Mental illness is a heavy burden in itself – we don't need attitude from others too.

'Now I've learnt to say no to people's outrageous demands and set boundaries of what I can achieve in one day. I exercise regularly and I eat well. All women can do these things to help themselves. Work culture is important too. It's good if employers encourage physical fitness which is closely linked to mental wellbeing. If people go to the gym in their lunchtime they shouldn't have to feel that colleagues are raising their eyebrows. Rather it should be seen as a positive sign of self-care.

'I had depression again at 44, but because of exercise (which I continued whilst depressed!), acupuncture, massage and the support of good friends, I did not need to go into hospital and the episode was much milder.'

Trisha Goddard's story

Trisha Goddard, 45, presents her own show for Granada TV: 'I started encountering bouts of depression from the age of 14, though it wasn't diagnosed until I was in the acute wing of a psychiatric ward in Sydney aged 37. Until then I'd done what many people do, lurched from one way of coping to another – frequent marijuana use, obsessive dieting and heavy drinking. I also kept getting into awful abusive relationships because I was so detached. I had two suicide attempts but it was only after the second that people took notice.

'I saw a psychiatrist twice a week after that and discovered I was a stereotype of the "smiling depressive" – in other words not the bleakly down and withdrawn depressive but some-one who is hyper-active, busy non-stop, often very talkative and uninhibited. We are the ones who when we go, go with such a bang that we self-combust.

'My sister had schizophrenia but that wasn't what killed her – it was the stigma. With the stigma come ignorance and fear and people have personal life choices taken away from them'

'My family has a predisposition to mental health problems – my aunt has lived with bi-polar disorder for much of her life and I had a sister with schizophrenia who burnt herself to death in 1988. I was working in Australia at the time and came back to England to be with her for the six weeks it took her to die. Trying to explain to people back in Australia why I'd dashed over here, without mentioning mental health, seemed not only to deny my sister's struggles but to deny her very existence. That's when I decided to tell people about the mental health problems in my family.

'Secrets and lies will destroy you every time. If I hadn't "come out" safely to a journalist in Australia after I ended up in a psychiatric wing I'd be tip-toeing around today coping with the added stress of secrets and lies. My sister had schizophrenia but that wasn't what killed her – it was

the stigma. With the stigma come ignorance and fear and people have personal life choices taken away from them.

'I've been very lucky with my employers. When I was headhunted by Anglia Television I explained to my boss that I lived with mental illness and therefore needed time for myself; as a result I've been allowed to arrange my days to safeguard my good health.

'Nowadays I always talk about living with depression because I've

managed to create the circumstances whereby I don't have to suffer any more. I've learnt what I need: for instance I've got an obsessive side which instead of fighting I now use productively by taking masses of exercise. I've also learnt that I'm not good in cities – I need the woods for my soul – so we moved to the countryside.

'My husband and two daughters are my care team and we have a contract that if they see me start becoming a bit frantic and detached they bring it to my attention. In order for them to feel secure I'll act on their concerns even if I'm convinced I'm not "skidding". I accept that they are the experts. And now so am I.'

■ The above information is from an article from Everywoman, the leading online network and resource provider for women business owners. Visit their web site which can be found at www.everywoman.co.uk

© Everywoman Ltd

The Bruno effect

Does the *Sun*'s climbdown after protests from readers mean that public attitudes to mental health problems are really changing?

The *Sun* has joined the UK's leading mental health charities, the Royal College of Psychiatry and the Department of Health in lending its support to people with mental health problems.

The newspaper announced on 25th September 2003 that it was launching a support fund – not as a result of long-term browbeating over the plight of the mentally ill, but following a storm of protest from readers over a headline about Frank Bruno in the early edition of 23 September: 'Bonkers Bruno locked up'. In later editions this was changed to: 'Sad Bruno in mental home'; and the former boxer was called a hero.

Is the *Sun*'s climbdown an acknowledgement that it had misjudged the public mood about mental health? Or is it simply a case of the paper underestimating the esteem in which Bruno is held?

The evidence of a shift towards greater compassion is mixed. A survey published by the Department of Health in June – the seventh since 1993 to examine public attitudes to mental health – found that attitudes became slightly worse between 2000 and 2003. Of those questioned, 89%

By Diane Taylor

said that society had a responsibility to provide people with mental health problems with the best possible care, a drop from 94% in 2000; 83% said society needed to adopt a more tolerant attitude; and 78% thought the mentally ill had for too long been the subject of ridicule.

Of 515 people living in England who took part in the survey 73% felt that media coverage of mental health issues over the previous three years had been unfair, unbalanced or very negative

Another survey conducted by the Office for National Statistics (ONS) for the Royal College of Psychiatrists in 1998, to launch its five-year Changing Minds campaign,

found that people with problems such as schizophrenia and addiction were often perceived as dangerous; the public had little sympathy for problems, such as eating disorders, that were seen to be self-inflicted; and people with mental health problems were seen as being difficult to communicate and empathise with.

The ONS has just completed another survey asking identical questions, revealing improvements in attitudes to many mental health issues, such as depression and dementia. However, it suggests that feelings towards addiction have seen no such change. It seems that people are prepared to be sympathetic to those they perceive as suffering through no fault of their own but are harder on those seen as having brought problems on themselves.

The prevalence of mental illness doesn't seem to guarantee an enlightened response. The Royal College of Psychiatrists says that some form of mental health problem affects the equivalent of one person in every family in the UK, while the mental health charity Sane says that one in 100 people suffers a serious mental breakdown.

And yet prejudices abound. A survey in 2000 by the Mental Health Foundation found that 37% of people with mental health problems said they had faced discrimination while looking for work; 47% had faced discrimination at work; and 55% didn't dare tell colleagues about their experience of mental distress. A previous survey for Mind found that more than a third of respondents had lost jobs because of their psychiatric history; 38% had been harassed, intimidated or teased at work.

The plethora of campaigns launched to elicit greater sensitivity towards people with mental health problems is another indication of just how far there is to go in terms of enhancing public awareness. Along with the Changing Minds campaign launched by the Royal College of Psychiatrists, the Department of Health has launched Mind out for Mental Health. It too is keen to reduce the stigma attached to such problems, and in partnership with the National Institute for Mental Health in England and other organisations, it hopes to stop the discrimination that surrounds them.

The use of words such as 'bonkers' in the *Sun* can inflict great pain on those who are mentally ill. The ripples go far beyond political correctness and for some can leave deep scars. Research by the mental health charity Mind carried out in 2000 found that negative and unbalanced media coverage actually increases mental health problems.

Of 515 people living in England who took part in the survey – including those with depression and anxiety, schizophrenia, manic depression and personality disorders – 73% felt that media coverage of mental health issues over the previous three years had been unfair, unbalanced or very negative; 50% of all respondents said that media coverage had a negative effect on their mental health; 34% felt more anxious and depressed; and 8% felt more suicidal.

While the latest statistical information about public attitudes to mental health is not entirely consistent, the Mind research shows how damaging negative media coverage can be. However, the *Sun's* climbdown and the kerfuffle about the issue shows that change is possible. The *Sun* has the dubious distinction of winning Mind's Bigot of the Year award three times – more than any other newspaper – but perhaps it won't win it again.

Tabloid newspapers do not include racist terms in their headlines simply because it is unacceptable to do so. With sustained campaigning, other minority groups can work towards eliminating the prejudiced terminology that refers to them.

It is sad to hear about Frank Bruno, but perhaps it will be of comfort to him that out of something so painful may come a more progressive attitude towards mental illness from a quarter where it was least expected.

© *Guardian Newspapers Limited 2003*

Mental illness

Information from the Mental Health Foundation

When someone experiences severe or enduring mental health problems they are sometimes described as 'mentally ill'. However, there are certain difficulties with this term.

- First, there is no universally agreed cut-off point between normal behaviour and that described as 'mental illness'. What is considered abnormal behaviour or an abnormal reaction to circumstances differs between cultures, social groups within the same culture, and even different social situations.

- Second, the label 'mental illness' is highly stigmatising. It encourages people to think of 'the mentally ill' as an entirely separate category from 'people like us', rather than as ordinary people who have, for whatever reason, more severe emotional difficulties to cope with. Popular misconceptions, fuelled by the media, depict 'the mentally ill' as violent and dangerous. These stereotypes are contradicted by ordinary people's experiences of mental health problems affecting themselves, their family members, friends or work colleagues.

- Third, use of the term mental illness may be misleading if it is taken to imply that all mental health problems are solely caused by medical or biological factors. In fact, most mental health problems result from a complex interaction of biological, social and personal factors. For example, some people may be biologically vulnerable to experiencing depression, yet strong social support during difficult times can reduce their risk of becoming severely depressed. Similarly, in people with a higher than average genetic risk of schizophrenia, a particular psychotic experience may be triggered by stressful life events and circumstances.

- Fourth, for many people the existing systems of categorising illnesses do not relate closely enough to their experiences. Some people, including some professionals, prefer not to accept diagnoses which may be misleading or stigmatising, for example 'personality disorder' or 'schizophrenia'. They find these terms unhelpful and prefer to talk about 'psychotic experiences'.

If you are interested in this subject, you may also find it useful to look at:
- *Mental health problems*. Factsheet. Mental Health Foundation, 2000.
- *Attitudes towards mental health problems*. Factsheet. Mental Health Foundation, 2000.

- The above information is from the Mental Health Foundation's web site which can be found at www.mentalhealth.org.uk

© *Mental Health Foundation*

Mental health in the workplace

About mental health and mental illness

Dispelling some myths about mental illness

There are many misconceptions about mental health problems, often fuelled by sensationalist media coverage. Research carried out by the Royal College of Psychiatrists in 1998[1] revealed that 30 per cent of employers interviewed would not, under any circumstances, consider employing people who had experienced mental health problems. This is a reflection of the large-scale lack of knowledge and understanding about mental illness.

Myth: All people with mental health problems are violent.

Reality: Mental illness is not a predictor of violence. With rare exceptions, the vast majority of people who have been diagnosed as having a mental health problem are not violent or aggressive in the workplace. Only one per cent of violent crimes committed against the person are by people assessed as having a mental disorder.[2] People with schizophrenia are 100 times more likely to harm themselves than to harm others, with a suicide rate of six to ten per cent[3] and they are more likely to be victimised as a result of their mental health.

Myth: Having a mental health problem will affect a person's ability to work reliably. (This is illustrated by a research study which found that a person with depression had significantly reduced chances of employment compared to someone with diabetes because of concerns about poor work performance.[4])

Reality: There is no reason to expect a person with mental health problems to be less reliable than anyone else. Some people's reliability will depend on the reasonable adjustments made – for example, someone who has problems with timekeeping may become a more reliable employee when flexible working hours are agreed.

Myth: Someone with a mental health problem is going to take lots of time off sick.

Reality: People may need time off with mental distress – but this is not always the case. In fact, people with a diagnosis of a severe mental illness may have excellent sickness records, and employment can contribute to their recovery and staying well. One supported employment programme within a mental health trust reports better sickness rates among people with a diagnosis of mental illness (3.8 per cent) than those of the rest of the organisation (5.8 per cent).[5] People with mental illness are often far more conscientious and motivated to 'do well' than others.[6]

Myth: People with a mental health problem are not going to be able to cope with the pressures and hold down a responsible job.

Reality: It would be incorrect to assume a person with mental health problems will not cope with a lot of responsibility. For many people, having a mental illness will have no effect on job performance; for others, it may only affect work temporarily. As with any employee, you need to explore strategies for managing work pressures and help them put these into practice. Be clear about the demands of the job and the support the organisation can provide.

Myth: Mental health problems are permanent and untreatable.

Reality: Studies over a significant period show that the majority of people with a mental health problem lead stable and productive lives.

References:

1 Leeds Mental Health Employment Strategy, Leeds Mental Health Employment Consortium, p3
2 Home Office figures for year ending June 1997
3 Bluglass and Bowden (Eds) (1990) Principles and Practice of Forensic Psychiatry, Churchill Livingstone
4 N. Glozier (1998) reported in the Royal College of Psychiatrists' Annual Meeting
5 South West London & St George's Mental Health NHS Trust (1999) Pathfinder User Employment Programme Progress Report, July 1999
6 Department of Health (1995) ABC of Health Promotion in the Workplace, Health Information Service

■ The above information is from Mental Health in the Workplace, one of a series of factsheets commissioned by the Greater London Authority and written by mentality.

© mentality

Emotional health and wellbeing

www.mindbodysoul.gov.uk

Who is normal?

Why is it that we are happy discussing our physical aches and pains but not so keen to talk about our mental health? The truth is, our mental wellbeing is just as important as our physical health.

Most people experience mental distress at some time, and it can affect your ability to handle day-to-day problems and enjoy life. The distress can be caused by a wide range of life events, such as school stresses, relationship problems or the death of someone close, which can all happen to anyone at any time.

As a teenager you have to cope with many changes, both physical and emotional and you need the support of friends and family to help you through. You will be faced with growing independence, mood swings, new anxieties, and the development of sexual and emotional awareness. Self-image is really important too. The way you feel about your looks, body shape and size, and how you think other people see you affects your self-esteem. Sometimes these problems get 'on top of you' and are hard to cope with.

We all get sad, angry or stressed out sometimes, so try to chill out when you don't feel good. Mental distress is common and can happen to anyone, so if you feel you really can't cope you're not alone. It's also not your fault, so don't feel guilty or under pressure to 'pull yourself together'. After all, if we didn't experience the bad times, we couldn't appreciate the good ones half as well.

The important thing to remember is that these problems are very common and you are not alone – and there are loads of things you can do to help.

Positive steps

Life is not always easy. There will always be stresses like exams, your love life, family and friends – that's life. If you can find ways of dealing with your stress in a positive way, then you will be helping yourself to look after your mental health.

What can children and young people do?

There are many different positive things that young people can do to help look after their own mental health. Different things will work for different people. So you need to find what works for you. The following are a few suggestions of some positive ways for dealing with emotions and stress.

Being creative

Activities such as drawing, painting, photography, writing, playing an instrument, singing, acting, and dancing can be good ways of expressing your feelings.

Letting out your emotions

Let people know how you feel. Talk to close friends and family members, and to your teacher. Bottling up feelings only creates more problems.

Taking time for yourself

Take time to listen to music, read a book, see a film, or have a relaxing bath. Or whatever it takes to help you think about things.

Getting out and about

Seeing friends is good for your mental health. Also, you could join a local group, or get involved in an after-school activity. You can find information about local groups from your local public library, or ask your teacher.

Getting active

Exercise is a good way of dealing with your stress, as well as being good for your physical health. It can also be a good way of meeting new people. Find out what's on offer at your local leisure centre and sign up!

Get help

There is usually a counselling service in most towns and sometimes in schools. If you do not think this type of service will suit you, you may be able to get information about other services which are available locally. There are often helpful posters in GP surgeries and health centres, also local phone books can be a useful source. If you cannot find what you are looking for on your own, ask – a teacher, school nurse, mentor or the social services office.

■ The above information is from the Department of Health's Mind, Body and Soul web site which can be found at www.mindbodysoul.gov.uk

© Crown copyright

Mental disorders

Challenging prejudice

Stigma: A mark of disgrace or infamy. Oxford English Dictionary

For centuries people with mental illness were kept away from the rest of society, sometimes locked up, often in poor conditions, with little or no say in running their lives. Today, negative attitudes lock them out of society more subtly but just as effectively.

Mental disorders affect everyone

Chances are you know someone who has or has had a mental health problem. Mental disorders – like anxiety, depression, eating disorders, drug and alcohol misuse, dementia and schizophrenia – can affect anyone, from any walk of life. In fact, they cause more suffering and disability than any other type of health problem.

Despite this, people with these conditions often attract fear, hostility and disapproval rather than compassion, support and understanding. Such reactions not only cause them to feel isolated and unhappy, but may also prevent them obtaining effective help and treatment.

In this article we turn the spotlight on the damaging effects of negative attitudes to mental disorders, and provide information about what we know about them. We hope to challenge you to think in new ways about mental disorders, and banish some of the myths and prejudices surrounding them.

The Royal College of Psychiatrists' campaign, Changing Minds: Every Family in the Land, aims to increase understanding of six common mental disorders, to challenge preconceptions about them, and to close the gap between what health professionals and the public perceive as useful treatments.
'Mental health is a key component of a healthy active life.'

Our Healthier Nation. Government Green Paper, 1998

What are mental disorders?

The term 'mental disorder' covers a wide range of different conditions affecting the mind. Mental disorders cause symptoms such as emotional upset, disturbed behaviour and poor memory. Sometimes illness elsewhere in the body disturbs the mind; at other times hidden mental upset may fuel other bodily disease or produce physical symptoms.

What causes mental disorders?

A whole range of different factors – our genetic blueprint, brain chemistry, aspects of our lifestyle, things that have happened to us in the past and our relationships with others – play a part. But whatever the cause, people who develop mental disorders often feel distressed, helpless and unable to lead their lives to the full.

Can mental disorders be treated?

The good news is that there are many effective treatments for mental disorders. These may include drugs and other physical treatments, talking treatments (psychotherapy) of various kinds, counselling and/or supporting people in their everyday lives in various ways.

A number of different professionals, medical and non-medical, may be involved in helping people who are mentally ill: GPs, psychiatrists, psychotherapists, counsellors, social workers, and voluntary user and self-help groups.

Psychiatry provides a diagnostic approach that allows the natural course of disorders to be known and predicted, and the effects of treatment to be more readily assessed.

What do psychiatrists do?

Psychiatrists are trained doctors who specialise in diagnosing and treating mental disorders.

A psychiatrist will examine the host of different factors that may have contributed to someone becoming mentally ill and try to tailor treatment as closely as possible to his or her individual needs.

Psychiatrists are qualified to provide a range of different treatments, including medication with drugs and/or different types of psychotherapy, often in partnership with other healthcare professionals. Psychiatrists are also licensed, by law, to recommend compulsory detention ('sectioning') in a mental health unit. This step is only taken in the interests of someone's health or safety or for the protection of others, and if their condition in these respects is very serious and yet they will not accept appropriate medical advice. Psychiatrists are unfortunately thus sometimes regarded as jailers, rather than as doctors with the interests of their patients in mind.

How can psychiatry help?

The causes of mental ill health are complex and psychiatrists don't have all the answers. As doctors, they are aware that some aspects of mental disorder, such as anxiety, despair and suicidal feelings, are not always easy to pin down.

'Changing Minds: Every Family in the Land' will point out some of the limitations to our knowledge and skill. However, we believe that by offering a systematic and scientific approach, psychiatry has an important part to play, involving both physical and psychological treatments, in relieving the suffering of people with mental disorders.

What is stigma?

In ancient Greece bodily signs or 'stigmata' were cut and burnt onto people's bodies to mark them as different. People with mental disorders are no longer physically mutilated, but critical or derogatory attitudes can be just as damaging to them. You only have to open a newspaper, switch on the TV or go to the cinema to spot such attitudes. While the media aren't wholly to blame for negative perceptions, every time a programme, article or film portrays a stereotype or fails to clear up a misunderstanding about a mental disorder, it helps to perpetuate the myths.

Where does stigma come from?

Stigma can arise in many ways. Mentally ill people may behave differently: a depressed person will appear sad or dull; someone who is in the elated (manic) phase of manic-depression may be unnaturally happy or irritable. Other factors, such as being seen visiting a psychiatric hospital or clinic may also mark someone as 'mental' or 'psychiatric'.

Why does it matter?

The trouble is, once someone is identified as different, it's hard for them to be accepted – no matter how hard they try. They can't shake off the stigma and as a result they lose confidence in themselves. In time they come to believe that they are odd and don't fit in.

Time for a change of mind

People with mental disorders continue to experience prejudice and discrimination in every area of their lives, from finding somewhere to live to getting a job. It's hardly surprising that many people with serious mental illness end up poor or homeless. It is up to all of us to become aware of the harm we do with our negative attitudes and to do our bit to stamp them out. Whoever we are and whatever we do, we can combat the harmful effects of stigma by extending our friendship, support and understanding, rather than our judgement and discrimination, to people who are mentally ill.

Fact or fiction?

Fiction
Describing people with mental disorders as 'loony', 'crackers', 'mad', 'barmy' or 'nuts' dismisses them as people not to be taken seriously, whilst the perception that they are dangerous – 'psycho' or 'schizo' – can result in them being excluded from everyday activities.

In fact, people with mental disorders need our compassion. Labels like these prevent true understanding

Fiction
Many people believe mental disorders are incurable. They may even view some treatments, like anti-depressants or psychotherapy, as useless or harmful – even though in many cases they have been proved to be effective.

In fact, mental disorders are treatable and are as likely to respond favourably to medical and other treatments as many physical illnesses. But the stigma of mental illness can make it harder for sufferers to seek help and more difficult for other people to help them.

Fiction
People with mental disorders are sometimes viewed as weak, as self-indulgent or as bringing their problems upon themselves. Even people with mental illness may believe they have themselves to blame.

In fact, people with mental disorders need you to recognise that they are ill as much as people with physical complaints.

Fiction
People with mental disorders often feel isolated and left out because other people imagine they are difficult to get on with.

In fact, people with mental disorders need friendship and understanding just like anyone else.

The future

Scientists are making progress in unravelling the structure and chemistry of the brain. As a result we have a better understanding of the mind and how it works. However, mental illness has many causes. It's not simply a matter of disturbed chemistry.

The new discoveries raise many questions to do with the nature of choice and responsibility. We still have a great deal we need to learn and understand.

Acknowledgements

We would like to thank Dr V. Y. Allison-Bolger and Dr R. L. Ramsay for their tremendous help in writing this information.

■ The Royal College of Psychiatrists' Changing Minds Campaign is part of a national movement to try and reduce the stigma of mental illness. Visit their web site for further information: www.rcpsych.ac.uk

© 2004 Royal College of Psychiatrists

Descriptions of mentally ill people

Statements to describe a person who is mentally ill

	Usually describes a person who is mentally ill	Might sometimes apply	Total mentions
Someone who has serious bouts of depression	55%	8%	63%
Someone who is incapable of making simple decisions about his or her own life	32%	11%	43%
Someone who has a split personality	53%	9%	61%
Someone who is born with some abnormality affecting the way the brain works	47%	8%	55%
Someone who cannot be held responsible for his or her own actions	45%	10%	55%
Someone prone to violence	29%	11%	40%
Someone who is suffering from schizophrenia	56%	8%	64%
Someone who has to be kept in a psychiatric or mental hospital	47%	9%	56%

Attitudes to Mental Illness in Great Britain: February 2003, Department of Health, Crown copyright

Positive steps to mental health

Information from mentality

What individuals can do

Stressed, anxious, worried or afraid?

Most of us feel like this from time to time. We may also have experiences that are very difficult to cope with. Losing someone you love or a relationship breaking up, being bullied, losing your job, sexual or racial harassment, or experiencing discrimination because of a mental health problem. Not having a voice because you're too young, too old or simply different. Doing something positive can make all the difference – for you and others.

Talking about it

Most people feel isolated and overwhelmed by their problems sometimes – it can help to share your feelings. If you feel there is no one to talk to, you could call a helpline.

Getting involved

Meeting new people and getting involved in things can make all the difference – for you and others.

Keeping active

Regular exercise really helps if you're feeling depressed or anxious. It can give you more energy too. Find something you enjoy – sport, swimming, walking, dancing or cycling.

Drinking in moderation

Drinking alcohol to deal with problems will only make things worse. It's best to drink in moderation and avoid binges, but if you're worried about your drinking speak to your doctor.

Learning new skills

Learning a new skill can increase your confidence – whether it's for pleasure, to make new friends or to improve your chances of a job.

Doing something creative

All kinds of creative things can help if you are anxious or low. They can also increase your confidence. Music, writing, painting, drawing, poetry, cooking, gardening – experiment to find something you enjoy.

Asking for help

Everyone needs help from time to time. It's OK to ask for help, even though it feels difficult – whether it's from friends and family, or from your local doctor, practice nurse, support group, faith community or helpline.

What communities/ organisations can do

Strengthening the mental wellbeing of communities involves increasing social inclusion and participation, improving neighbourhood environments, developing health and social services which support mental health, anti-bullying strategies at school, workplace health, community safety, childcare, self-help networks and so on.

The following 12-point plan is based on current evidence of effectiveness. Many other approaches may be equally valuable, but may not yet have been evaluated or included in the research literature.

Employers can:

- Introduce a mental health promotion policy at work
  – mental health and wellbeing of staff
  – support for their returning to work after a mental health problem
  – positive approach to employment of people with mental health problems.

Local authorities can:

- Increase access to green open spaces.

Local authorities, sports and leisure clubs and primary care can:

- Increase opportunities for and access to exercise.

Adult education, voluntary agencies and primary care can:

- Increase opportunities for and access to arts and creativity.

Local authorities, health authorities, primary care and voluntary agencies can:

- Support and promote self-help groups
- Support and promote volunteering
- Provide support, home visits and parenting skills for pregnant women and new parents.

Schools can:

- Become a Health Promoting School
- Introduce an anti-bullying policy at school.

Strategic health authorities, primary care trusts and teams can:

- Offer training in cognitive behavioural therapy, which is more effective than generic counselling.

Primary care can:

- Ask about alcohol consumption and offer information and advice to people drinking above the recommended levels.

Strategic health authorities and mental health services can:

- Increase the social inclusion of people with long-term mental health problems.

■ The above information is from mentality's web site which can be found at www.mentality.org.uk

© 2004 mentality

About mental illness

What is mental illness?

Missed the train or started a new job? Stress is a part of everyday life: it simply means that you feel threatened and have to find ways of adapting or coping. Stress over a long period of time, however, may affect your physical and mental health.

We expect people to behave in a particular way depending on the context. If you shout and fling yourself around on the morning bus in the same way as a reveller in a club, you are thought not to be yourself.

When a person cannot cope with the everyday demands of life or presents a danger to themselves or others, they are often described as being mentally ill. 15% of the UK population will experience a mental illness such as depression, schizophrenia or phobia during their lifetime. Such illnesses involve subtle changes in the way that brain cells communicate. Imbalances in the chemical 'ferries' between neurons lead to changes and confusion in cell signalling.

Because mental illness can be very difficult to define, we are a long way from understanding its causes. Genes, the environment, life experience and chemistry may all play a part.

What are the steps to take?

Seeking help from family and friends is probably the best first step if you are feeling depressed, anxious or stressed. Often sympathy and understanding is all you need. And if you know someone going through a difficult time it is worth bearing this in mind. Making judgements and commenting on their situation to everyone else won't help.

It is not very helpful to talk about someone in this situation as neurotic, psychotic, schizophrenic or manic depressive. These terms describe severe mental illnesses and shouldn't really be used in a general way.

Who else can help?

If you have talked with your family, friends, teacher, adviser at college, youth worker or whoever you trust with your feelings, and you still don't feel right, it is best to make an appointment with your GP. Your GP may put you in touch with a support organisation like the Samaritans or CRUSE (a bereavement service for people who have lost someone close to them) or with local social services and family health service staff.

If this step doesn't seem successful and others around you still feel you need help social services and community health workers may arrange a meeting to find out what is wrong. They will talk to you about what the options are. It may be that your family will be involved and be given support as well. You may meet with others in groups to talk about your situation. Some young people are asked to keep a diary of their feelings or their behaviour.

They can be taught how to change the things about themselves which they don't like. Young people with problems which are difficult to manage may be offered certain medicines or the chance to go into a hospital.

Will anyone need to know if you have asked a professional for help?

One of the biggest concerns about mental health is that people asking for advice, either for themselves or on behalf of others, will be labelled as having a problem. Information given to a GP or anyone else in the health or education services is confidential. This means that others, even other members of your family, cannot see confidential information.

It may be that you will be asked to have a medical examination at some point. If you are 16 or over you may agree yourself to a medical examination and treatment. Even if you are younger than this you should be consulted and asked about treatment as long as you are capable of giving informed consent.

- Get some exercise or go for a walk in the fresh air;
- Maintain a healthy, balanced diet;
- Don't worry too much about not sleeping well. Try some relaxation techniques, milky drinks or reading before sleeping;
- Drowning your sorrows with alcohol will not help – it is a depressant drug and you may end up feeling worse.

■ The above information is from the National Youth Agency's web site: www.youthinformation.com
© *National Youth Agency*

Treatment of children and teenagers

Treatment in childhood could halve rates of mental disorders

Up to half of all cases of adult mental disorder could be prevented by the effective treatment of children and teenagers with psychiatric disorders. This is the conclusion of a study carried out at the Institute of Psychiatry.

Most adults with a psychiatric disorder had a diagnosable disorder as children, according to the study, published in the *Archives of General Psychiatry* this week. In fifty per cent of cases this first diagnosis was between the ages of 11 and 15.

The study was carried out by Prof Terrie Moffitt, Dr Julia Kim-Cohen and Prof Avshalom Caspi in collaboration with colleagues in New Zealand. 1037 people born between 1 April 1972 and 31 March 1973 in Dunedin, New Zealand, took part in the study, which forms part of the Dunedin Multi-disciplinary Health and Development Study.

The mental health of the participants was assessed every two to three years from the age of eleven using the Diagnostic Interview Schedule (DIS) and the DIS for Children, commonly used psychiatric assessment tools. The rates of childhood mental disorders were examined in adults with a range of psychiatric conditions and compared with rates amongst participants with no psychiatric symptoms.

Childhood mental disorders examined included depression, anxiety and Attention Deficit Hyperactivity Disorder (ADHD). ADHD is a persistent pattern of poor attention and/or overactive, impulsive behaviour. Also examined were rates of conduct disorder and oppositional defiant disorder. Conduct disorder is characterised by aggressive behaviour that causes or threatens physical harm to others, destructive behaviour, deceitfulness or theft, and serious violations of rules. Children with oppositional

defiant disorder have difficulty following rules and behaving in a socially acceptable way.

The team found that:
- 26% of adult anxiety disorder might have been prevented if childhood depression, ADHD, conduct and/or oppositional defiant disorder, and anxiety had been effectively treated
- 23% of adult depression might have been prevented if childhood anxiety, depression and conduct and/or oppositional defiant disorder had been effectively treated
- 25% of adult schizophrenia-type disorders such as schizophrenia and psychosis might have been prevented if childhood depression, anxiety, conduct and/or oppositional defiant disorder and ADHD had been effectively treated
- 32% of adult mania might have been prevented if childhood depression and conduct and/or oppositional defiant disorder had been effectively treated
- 46% of adult eating disorders might have been prevented if childhood conduct and/or oppositional defiant disorder had been effectively treated
- 41% of adult antisocial personality disorder might have been prevented if childhood conduct and/or oppositional defiant disorder had been effectively treated

Currently few children with psychiatric conditions receive treatment. The report's authors call for screening by GPs and in schools to detect children with psychiatric conditions and provide appropriate treatment. Such preventative methods could reduce the rate of adult mental disorder by up to 46%.

This article is a summary of: Kim-Cohen J, Caspi A, Moffitt TE, Harrington H, Milne BJ, Poulton R. 'Prior Juvenile Diagnoses in Adults With Mental Disorder – Developmental Follow-Back of a Prospective-Longitudinal Cohort, 2003.' *Archives of General Psychiatry.* 60 pp709-717.

- The above information is from Mental Health Care's web site: www.mentalhealthcare.org.uk

Mental health in education

Information from the British Association for Counselling and Psychotherapy

Introduction/the issue

Many schools already make the emotional health of their students a priority but as a profession we can do more.

A significant number of children and young people in school are experiencing a range of mental health problems along a continuum stretching from the mild and transitory to the severe, but these sometimes go largely unnoticed by staff in schools whose focus by necessity lies primarily with formal achievement and meeting externally set targets and expectations.

There is evidence to show that students in our schools are depressed, stressed and anxious. We see an increase in the incidence of self-harming behaviours and suicidal thoughts and actions. Recent research by the NCH has revealed that 1 in 17 adolescents may be self-harming, with respondents suggesting that schools and parents had been ill prepared in terms of help that they could offer. Perhaps even more shocking is the fact, revealed by the NSPCC, that suicide has overtaken road accidents as the main cause of death among young people in Northern Ireland.

Eating disorders are on the increase as are the numbers of children simply unable to face the pressures of going to school. Some young people will inevitably go on to develop more profound and longer-term mental illnesses. Where problems do occur, the school's response is often to address overt behaviours especially where these affect the teaching and learning of others in the school. Where greater emotional problems exist, the school may elicit the help of psychologists, social workers or mental health professionals. These responses are essentially reactive.

Although an inter-agency approach can produce good results, there is much to be gained by schools taking a more proactive stance. This

British Association for Counselling and Psychotherapy

means a move towards early identification of problems, early intervention and support at key moments in the lives of young people. I am advocating a pre-emptive approach, which anticipates problems and which offers not only individual support but also addresses issues of mental health through the curriculum and through the wider school organisation and ethos.

As a professional working in education, mental health and counselling, I have dealt with young people experiencing emotional distress; I have observed the consequences for those whose difficulties remained unseen or which manifested themselves in ways that elicited a less than sympathetic response.

The extent of the problem

Mental health problems in young people are a clear predictor of difficulties in adulthood.[1] Acknowledging the extent of the problem increases awareness and enables action to be taken as soon as symptoms are identified.

- In any secondary school of 1,000 pupils there are likely to be:[2] 50 pupils who are seriously depressed; 100 in significant distress; 10-20 pupils with OCD; and 5-10 girls with an eating disorder.
- 10-20 per cent of young people involved in criminal activity are thought to have a 'psychiatric disorder'.
- Suicide by young men has increased by 75 per cent in 10 years.[3]
- Every day more than 400 children receive in-depth counselling by ChildLine.[4]

Schools are uniquely placed to play a central role alongside other agencies and professionals in promoting and sustaining young people's emotional health. A concern for young people's mental health in schools is of course wholly compatible with a school's primary concern for providing a quality education. Indeed, I would argue that to ignore the emotional dimension to schooling and not make children's mental health a priority could seriously undermine school success and student achievement.

This article provides information about mental health difficulties experienced by young people and gives practical guidance on routes to seeking help. It will also hopefully raise awareness of some of the issues, promote discussion and dialogue and ultimately place children's emotional health and well-being at the centre of our educational agenda.

Some signs and symptoms of emotional and behavioural disorders

Emotional/physical

- Persistent sadness and hopelessness
- Poor self-esteem
- Feelings of guilt
- Frequent physical complaints, such as headaches and stomachaches
- Anger and rage, frequent temper tantrums
- Excessive weight loss or gain: obesity, anorexia nervosa, bulimia nervosa
- Hyperactivity
- Thoughts of death or suicide
- Thoughts of running away
- Extreme fear
- Persistent nightmares/dramatic changes in sleep patterns
- Wants to be alone all the time/ withdrawal from others
- Hears voices that cannot be explained
- Unable to get over a loss or death of someone important

- Chronic tiredness
- Soiling/wetting
- Phobias
- Anxiety
- Delay in acquiring skills such as speech
- Lack of enthusiasm, energy or motivation
- Inability to cope with problems and daily activities
- Overreaction to criticism

Behavioural
- Aggression, anti-social behaviour, bullying or threatening others
- Absenteeism or poor school performance
- Withdrawal from friends/activities
- Problems with authority
- Indecision, lack of concentration, forgetfulness
- Drug/alcohol abuse
- Harming animals
- Self-destructive behaviour: cutting, overdosing
- Performing certain routines in excess (OCD)
- Stealing
- Fire-setting

Existing resources and access to counselling

Some schools already have well-established in-school support systems to help pupils in difficulty.

Key roles and departments in school include:
- The school's pastoral system (which can include a counselling service) including head of year and form tutor
- Special needs department
- Learning mentors
- Learning support unit

External agencies for referrals include:
- School nurses
- GPs
- Educational welfare services
- Behaviour support services
- Connexions
- Social services
- Residential social workers
- Juvenile justice workers
- Parents/carers
- Community psychiatric services
- Clinical child psychologists

- Child psychiatrists
- Educational psychologists
- Community psychiatric nurses
- Occupational therapists
- Art, music and drama therapists
- Health visitors

Working with external agencies

School nurses, health visitors and GPs can be an important point of referral where there are concerns about a child's physical or psychological health. The Educational Welfare Services act as a link between home and school and can form a useful partnership with the school when a child is unable or unwilling to attend school. Social Services are of course the first point of referral where there are concerns about a child's physical, emotional or sexual safety or where the young person's problems are partially caused, or exacerbated, by family neglect.

Where a child is being 'looked after' it is often useful to establish close links with residential social workers. Similarly, where a young person has become involved in crime, delinquency or anti-social behaviour, juvenile justice workers are often more than willing to work closely with the school in the best interests of the student. LEA behaviour support services offer specialist input for young people who have associated behavioural problems and sometimes can access off-site provision.

The relatively new Connexions Service (www.connexions.gov.uk) is keen to work with schools and support young people in very practical ways during the latter years of secondary school, especially in relation to transition post-16.

Educational psychologists are normally accessed through the LEA and offer advice and guidance where learning and/or behavioural difficulties are contributing to the young person's problems. They are also crucial in the Statementing process, which enables young people and schools to access additional resources where a child's special educational needs have been clearly identified.

Where a child's problems are of a psychological nature, and are seen as established or acute, there are a number of professionals who may already be working with a school student, or who would be willing to become involved after an appropriate referral. These include: clinical psychologists, child psychiatrists, community psychiatric nurses, occupational therapists and other professionals who can be accessed through local Child and Adolescent Mental Health Services. In addition there are an increasing number of professionals working with young people, whose focus is a creative one and these include art, drama, music and play therapists.

Schools should not of course undervalue the potential benefits of a good working relationship with parents and guardians who can play a crucial part in a child's recovery and long-term emotional well-being. Where appropriate, family therapy can sometimes be accessed.

How counselling interacts with other agencies

Counselling can support the above agencies by offering a specific kind of support to young people with emotional problems. Counselling does not seek to replace other forms of support but can complement them in a highly-skilled, professional manner.

How counselling can be accessed

The most common models of counselling service delivery in schools are:
- In some areas the LEA provides the counselling service and it is centrally managed and resourced, with counsellors delivering the service to the schools in the area. These are sometimes employed

in the Inclusion or Additional Educational Needs Division. Some LEAs have developed a 'buy back' funding arrangement.

- In some areas the schools and LEAs link the services provided to other agencies such as health, social services and charitable organisations such as the National Society for Prevention of Cruelty to Children (NSPCC).

If you, your school or your Local Education Authority is considering setting up a counselling service or employing a counsellor, a free guide *Guidelines for Counselling in Schools* is available from the BACP Information Department on 0870 443 5252.

Schools should not undervalue the potential benefits of a good working relationship with parents and guardians

---

References
1. Achenbach, T.M. et al. (1995) Six-year predictors of problems in a national sample: III. Transitions to young adult syndromes *Journal of the American Academy of Child and Adolescent Psychiatry* 34: 658-669
2. Meltzer, H. et al. (2000) *Mental health of children and adolescents in Great Britain*. Office for National Statistics, London: The Stationery Office (www.statistics.gov.uk).
3. www.youngminds.org.uk
4. www.childline.org.uk

By Mark Prever, Manager, Student Support Centre, Yardleys School, Birmingham; Chair, Open Door Youth Counselling Agency, Birmingham; Chair, Counselling in Education – a Division of BACP

- The above information is from the British Association for Counselling and Psychotherapy's web site which can be found at www.bacp.co.uk

The saddest university challenge of all

Mental illness tests students and colleges

On a wet day five years ago, Rachael Tooth's mother drove her to Cardiff University to start the first term of a degree course in journalism, film and broadcasting. Rachael was full of enthusiasm for the enriching experience she imagined lay ahead.

She threw herself into student politics, and quickly acquired a set of friends with whom to share a house in her second year.

It was in the second year, when Rachael was living in substandard rented accommodation, that her mental health began a slow decline. She felt overwhelmed by her overdraft and, after excelling in her first year, was handing in essays that barely made sense.

When she stopped sleeping and started to have fantasies about drinking bleach, she asked her flatmates to hide all the chemicals and medicines.

More than 200 miles away, Rachael's family had little idea of her anguish, which she became adept at disguising. It was her closest friend who took her to the university counselling service and waited while she filled in a self-assessment form.

By Alexandra Buxton

'Asked what I was worried about, I said money and coursework,' she says. 'But the counsellor knew immediately that I was in a far worse state than I acknowledged.'

Recently, Rachael gave a courageous account of her experience of overcoming mental illness at a conference on student mental health organised by the Heads of University Counselling Services (HUCS).

Designed to highlight the importance of mental health support for students, the event was attended by counsellors from universities all over the United Kingdom, as well as from organisations such as the Samaritans.

As many as a third of university students suffer from some form of mental distress, which ranges from clinical disorders to temporary periods of anxiety and depression. About one in 10 undergraduates has one-to-one counselling.

'Studies show that students look first to family and friends,' says Colin Lago, director of counselling services at Sheffield University. 'It's often friends and family who suggest talking to the counselling service.'

In the past few years, counsellors have reported an increase in the number of students with serious mental health problems such as schizophrenia and manic depression.

Last year the percentage of students using counselling services who reported feeling suicidal rose from 10 per cent to 15 per cent.

Guided by Papyrus, a charity founded by parents to prevent young people killing themselves, Universities UK, the body that speaks for British universities, has published guidelines on reducing the risk of suicide.

Each year, about 150 students take their own lives; the number of young adults committing suicide across the country is about the same. Approximately three-quarters of student suicides are male.

'Counselling services need to develop ways of reaching male students, who account for only a third of their clients,' says Rita Rebholz, a member of Papyrus. 'Some universities already offer online counselling, which young men often prefer.'

By 2010 the Government wants half of all young people to enter higher education, but counsellors fear that support services will not cope with the extra numbers.

'Widening participation means that many students are struggling on both a personal and an academic level, which makes them vulnerable to anxiety and feelings of failure,' says Brian Kelly, head of counselling at the University of Luton.

The onset of mental health problems often coincides with life changes. So how can parents help children to make the challenging transition from home to university?

'Students newly arrived at university need their parents more, not less, than before, so it's good to stay in touch,' says Pauline McManus, head of the counselling service at Warwick University. 'Students need reassurance that nothing has changed at home.'

Rachael Tooth's parents separated, briefly, soon after she started university, adding to her sense of isolation. In her third year she was diagnosed with bipolar disorder, an illness characterised by emotional highs and lows.

With help from the counselling service, she negotiated a year's extension on her coursework. She got a good degree and now works for the Equal Opportunities Commission.

For Rachael, the counselling service at Cardiff University was, quite literally, a lifeline. She would like universities to offer better academic support to students with mental health problems.

'Given that mental health problems are so common, I think universities should train academic staff to understand the issues involved,' she says. 'I found myself explaining my illness to tutors in crowded corridors.'

■ Papyrus, Rossendale GH, Union Road, Rawstenstall, Lancs BB4 6NE (www.papyrus-uk.org).

Student mental health reminder

Leading charity issues mental health reminder to students

The Mental Health Foundation today (15 April 2003) issued a mental health reminder to students starting or returning to university this autumn. Research suggests that the prevalence and severity of mental illness in university students is increasing.

According to the Foundation, while many people have the time of their life at university, students experience higher than average levels of anxiety and depression. In a survey done by the Mental Health Foundation, clinically measurable anxiety was recorded in large numbers of students and 12% of male and 15% of female students experienced clinical depression (compared with one in ten of the general population).

Mental distress can occur when new students face a range of challenges like the transition from home to university life. Dealing with accommodation, fitting in and making friends, and managing time and finances can seem daunting, and even overwhelming.

It is not only first-time students who experience anxiety and depression, returning and mature students also have to juggle studies with paid work and are increasingly stressed trying to make ends meet. The average student can now expect to leave university with debt in the region of £12 -£15,000.

Annie Blunt, Head of Children and Young People's Mental Health at the Foundation, said:

'It's important to enjoy university as much as you can, but getting worried or depressed is pretty common too. Getting involved in activities and societies is a good idea, as is looking after yourself by watching your physical health. You need your sleep, good food, plenty of exercise, friends to talk to and not too much alcohol.

'Studying brings pressures around essays, assignments and exams. Wanting good results is natural but it's good to keep things in proportion and not lose sight of yourself as a whole person. You won't simply be judged on what you achieve academically.'

She also stressed the importance of talking to someone. Students can wait too long before seeking help for emotional and mental health problems. It is important for them to recognise when they need help and to seek it. Universities have support services such as welfare and counselling, personal tutors and some have peer-led services such as Niteline, run by students, for students.

Students should also speak to their GP if their problems are more acute. For example, if they are experiencing panic attacks, sleep or appetite disturbance and loss of concentration or serious thoughts of self-harm, GPs can help them to access appropriate professional support.

■ The information on this page was provided by the Mental Health Foundation Press Office. Visit their web site at www.mentalhealth.org.uk

Improved services for young people

World Mental Health Day 2003 to promote improved services for young people

The future of our society depends on the emotional health of our young people. However, many children have adolescent and behavioural problems that interfere with healthy development and functioning. Left unrecognised and untreated, many of these problems continue into adulthood and can severely limit educational, work and social achievement.

The World Health Organisation estimates that worldwide up to 20% of children and adolescents have a mental health disorder serious enough to need professional attention. Yet, fewer than one in five received needed treatment. It is possible that, by 2020, child and adolescent emotional and behavioural disorders could rise proportionately by fifty per cent throughout the world to become one of the five most common causes of death, illness and disability among children.

On 10 October 2003, World Mental Health Day, the global mental health education programme of the World Federation for Mental Health (WFMH) will launched a worldwide, year-long public awareness and advocacy campaign to focus increased attention on the needs of children and adolescents who are experiencing emotional and behavioural problems, promote the planning, funding and development of increased and improved mental health services for young people, and encourage citizen advocacy to support the adoption by national governments of child and adolescent mental health policies.

According to WFMH's President L. Patt Franciosi, 'Few national government policies designed specifically to support child and adolescent mental health exist worldwide. In fact, a recent survey of national mental health policies did not find a single country with a

mental health policy strictly pertaining to children and adolescents, although 34 countries were found to have identifiable mental health policies that may have some beneficial impact on children and adolescents. The absence of policy is a major barrier to the development of coherent systems of mental health care for children and adolescents.'

'The 2003 World Mental Health Day campaign theme focuses on emotional and behavioral disorders of children and adolescents', Dr Franciosi stated, 'because so many young people around the world are not receiving the attention they deserve. This year's campaign will help to increase worldwide awareness and advocacy concerning the devastating effects of emotional and

behavioural disorders on the lives of children and adolescents. We expect that public awareness, education and advocacy activities commemorating World Mental Health Day will be held in over 100 countries.'

2003 marks the eleventh year that the World Federation for Mental Health has organised the World Mental Health Day global mental health education campaign. WFMH is an international multidisciplinary organisation founded in 1948 to advance among all people and nations, the prevention of mental and emotional disorders, the proper treatment and care of those with such disorders, and the promotion of mental health.

■ Copies of the World Mental Health Day campaign packet can be obtained by contacting WFMH at wmhday@wfmh.com

■ The above information is from the World Federation for Mental Health's World Mental Health Day campaign. Visit their web site at www.wfmh.org

© *World Federation for Mental Health (WFMH)*

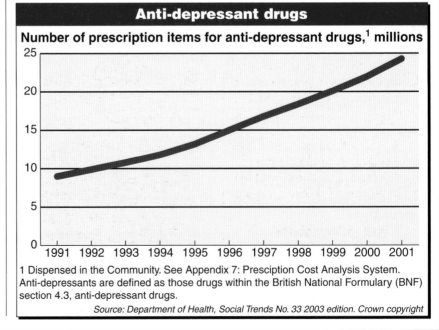

Anti-depressant drugs

Number of prescription items for anti-depressant drugs,[1] millions

1 Dispensed in the Community. See Appendix 7: Presciption Cost Analysis System.
Anti-depressants are defined as those drugs within the British National Formulary (BNF) section 4.3, anti-depressant drugs.

Source: Department of Health, Social Trends No. 33 2003 edition. Crown copyright

How to beat depression

Depression is a genuine illness. It is far better to seek appropriate help than just to be miserable. There are many different types of treatment available, which can be tailored to the type and severity of the illness. Here is a guide to the main types of treatments available for depression

Can I help myself?

Recognising that you are depressed and wanting to do something about it is an essential first step in fighting depression. Simply changing your lifestyle can often help. Take time to relax. Even though you may feel exhausted, take regular exercise, every day if possible.

Avoid snacking on sweet foods and cut down on coffee and alcohol. Eat a well-balanced diet, with plenty of fresh fruit and vegetables and a reasonable amount of protein. Eat regular meals, and have a milky, noncaffeinated drink at bedtime – it can help you get a good night's sleep.

Aromatherapy massage with essential oils of bergamot, lavender, rose, clary sage or ylang ylang can aid relaxation and lift mood. Homeopathic remedies that may help to lift mood include Ignatia, Pulsatilla, Natrum mur and Sulphur.

Is there an alternative to taking drugs?

There is good evidence that St John's Wort can be a very effective remedy for mild to moderate depression. It takes about two weeks to work. Many doctors recommend it, but they cannot prescribe it, so you will have to buy it from either a chemist or a health food shop.

If you are on other medication, ask the pharmacist or your doctor for advice. Unless advised by a doctor, pregnant women should not take St John's Wort.

St John's Wort is a good first choice remedy for mild depression, but if it does not appear to be working after a couple of weeks see your doctor.

Will talking about depression help?

Medication can help with the symptoms of depression but it does not tackle all the underlying problems. In general, the most effective types of therapy for depression are ones that focus on the 'here and now' (rather than the past) and on specific problems.

Cognitive behaviour therapy aims to change the way you think. CBT teaches you to recognise negative thoughts, and change them into more positive, realistic ones.

It can be very successful in treating depression and can help to prevent it recurring. It can be used either on its own or together with anti-depressants.

CBT is usually provided on a one-to-one basis by a trained psychotherapist. It is also newly available via a special computer program. CBT is widely available on the NHS, but waiting lists tend to be long.

Could drugs help?

Depression is associated with chemical changes in the brain. In particular, the brain responds less to the natural mood-enhancing chemicals serotonin and noradrenaline. Anti-depressant drugs increase the activity of these chemicals.

Unlike tranquillisers, such as Valium, anti-depressants are not

addictive. In general, only one type of anti-depressant should be taken at a time, but they can be used in conjunction with natural remedies or talking therapies. Your doctor will probably prescribe a course of drugs from one of the following three groups.

SSRIs

This group of drugs, the Selective Serotonin Reuptake Inhibitors, includes fluoxetine (Prozac), paroxetine (Seroxat) and sertraline (Lustral). They are very effective at treating depression, and can also help relieve anxiety and panic attacks. Side-effects can include an increase in anxiety during the first week of treatment, nausea, and, less commonly, feeling sleepy for a few hours after taking the tablet.

They can also affect sexual function, making it hard to reach orgasm. However, in general, side-effects are rare, and they are safer than other tri-cyclics if an overdose is taken. Some people feel dizzy if they stop SSRIs suddenly, so cut down slowly.

Tri-Cyclics

These include amitriptyline (Tryptizol), dothiepin (Prothiaden) and lofepramine (Gamanil). They are effective, and cheap, but usually take about three weeks to work. Side-effects, such as a dry mouth, drowsiness and constipation, are common. They can be dangerous if taken in overdose, and must be used carefully by people with certain medical conditions, such as epilepsy or some heart complaints. However, they can be a good choice for people who have sleep problems or who are depressed because of chronic pain.

MAOIs

The older type of monoamine oxidase inhibitor, such as Marplan and

Nardil, are now rarely used because they can be dangerous if taken with foods that contain tyramine, such as cheese, yeast extract and some types of red wine. Recently, a new type, known as RIMAs (reversible inhibitor of monoamine oxidase) has become available, where interaction with foods is less of a problem.

What if none of these treatments work?

A treatment called electro-convulsive therapy (ECT) is sometimes given to people who are severely depressed and have not responded to drug treatment.

The treatment involves the patient being given a general anaesthetic and then an electric current is passed through the sufferer's brain, causing a convulsion like an epileptic fit. It is a controversial treatment which can have severe side-effects such as memory loss. Around 10,000 people are prescribed ECT in Britain each year.

Is there a different type of treatment for manic depression?

Yes. Because manic depression involves the suffer experiencing both high – or manic – episodes and low moods traditional anti-depressants are not suitable because they may accentuate the high moods when they occur.

Instead drugs called mood stabilisers are used. The three main types are lithium, carbamazapine and sodium valproate. Drugs are the first line of treatment for manic depression. Cognitive behavioural therapy is also increasingly being used to help sufferers.

Can I relieve seasonal affective disorder without taking anti-depressants?

Yes, depending on the severity of your condition there is much you can do to help yourself without taking anti-depressants. Everything from exercise to getting outdoors to avoiding carbohydrates can help. Light therapy, which involves using special high intensity 'light boxes', is one of the main forms of treatment for SAD.

These boxes contain a light five to 20 times more intense than a well-lit office and help to rebalance the happy hormones in the brain, restoring mood. Light boxes are available in many shapes and sizes and can be used at home and in the office. They are available at most major chemists priced around £170. Some are even available for hire. For more details contact the SAD Association at www.sada.org.uk

Where can I get more help?

Depression Alliance provides information, support and understanding to anyone affected by depression. For a free information pack call 020 7633 0557, fax 020 7633 0559, e-mail information@depressionalliance.org or write to them at 35 Westminster Bridge Road, London, SE1 7JB (enclosing an SAE).

Call the Fellowship of Depressives Anonymous on 01702 433838 for support and encouragement for former depressives.

Call the Manic Depression Fellowship on 020 7793 2600 or visit their website: www.icmedicine.co.uk for help with manic depression.

For information on post-natal depression visit the Association For Postnatal Illness's website on www.apni.org

© *The Daily Mail, 2004*

Mental Health Bill – questions and answers

Legislation to reform mental health policy was not included in the Queen's speech for the second year running. David Batty explains

What is the draft Mental Health Bill?
The Bill sets out the government's proposed reforms of the 1983 Mental Health Act, which staff and service users have long argued is out of date. According to the Department of Health (DoH), it would remove a legal loophole that allows up to 600 dangerous people with severe mental disorders to avoid treatment by arguing that they gain no benefit from it. The legislation would also permit the compulsory treatment of mentally ill people being cared for in the community, as well as hospital patients.

Why has the government proposed reform of the current law?
The government first announced plans to detain psychopaths who have not committed a crime following-

---

The legislation would also permit the compulsory treatment of mentally ill people being cared for in the community, as well as hospital patients

---

ing the public outrage at the murder by Michael Stone of Lin Russell and her six-year-old daughter Megan in Kent in 1996. Stone had been left free to commit the crime because his severe personality disorder was considered untreatable and he could not be detained under the Mental Health Act. Ministers estimated there were up to 2,400 similar people in the UK, which they described as having dangerous and severe personality disorder (DSPD). Although the vast majority are held in prison or a secure mental hospital, 300-600 live in the community.

With regard to compulsory community treatment, the government says it wants to ensure that treatment reaches some of the most vulnerable service users who at the moment drift out of care too easily, become ill and need frequent admission to hospital.

What other proposals are included in the Bill?

It also contains new safeguards, which the government says will ensure that people who have never done anything wrong will not be detained on the speculative say-so of a psychiatrist. An independent tribunal will examine care plans for everyone detained for more than 28 days. At present this happens only if the patient lodges an appeal. The Bill will also introduce a right to independent advocacy to ensure that detained patients' interests are properly represented. It also proposes new safeguards to balance the rights of the child and the rights of their parents, by giving under-18s the right to refuse treatment. Currently children can in effect consent to treatment, but not refuse it. If they refuse, it can still go ahead if their parents consent. Another controversial measure is a duty for staff to co-operate in the supply of information, which appears to be a carte blanche to throw open patients' medical notes.

Why has the Bill proved so controversial?

Both professionals and service users wanted a new Bill to enshrine the right to assessment and treatment for people who wanted it and to reduce the amount of compulsion that already exists in the system. But the draft Bill is regarded as widely extending powers to enforce treatment and/or detain people with mental illness or personality disorder. The Bill revises the definition of 'mental disorder' to embrace 'any disability or disorder of the mind or brain, which results in impairment or disturbance of mental functioning'.

The 1983 Act's condition of 'treatability' would also be removed so that there would be no exclusion of people who suffer only from drug

or alcohol abuse or sexual deviancy, and no requirement to exhaust less restrictive options before resorting to compulsion.

Who was consulted about the Bill?

In 1998 the government commissioned an expert review of the Mental Health Act under Genevra Richardson, professor of law at Queen Mary and Westfield College, London, which recommended that any extension of compulsion should be balanced by improvement of rights and safeguards for the individual.

Although there are such improvements in the draft Bill, professionals and service users say they go nowhere near far enough. Critics argue that the services provided to an individual would be determined by the level of risk they pose to others rather than, as Prof Richardson proposed, the level of their mental capacity.

Which groups are opposed to the Bill?

The Bill has succeeded in uniting mental health professionals, charities and service users in condemnation of its proposals. Campaigners have set up the Mental Health Alliance (MHA), a coalition of more than 50 organisations including the mental health charities Mind, Sane and Rethink, the Law Society and the Royal College of Psychiatrists. The MHA is opposed to the Bill's 'draconian new powers of compulsion'.

What impact might the Bill have on attitudes towards mental illness?

Campaigners fear that the Bill's emphasis on managing risk will reinforce the public misconception that mentally ill people are dangerous. A knock-on effect of this would be to heighten the stigma surrounding mental illness. Research conducted for the charity Mind in September 2002 found that more than one in three members of the public would be deterred from seeking help from their GP for depression if the proposed Bill became law. The proportion rose to 52% among young people aged 15-24 who are particularly at risk from depression.

How has the government reacted to this criticism?

In the face of continued widespread opposition, the draft Bill was omitted from the Queen's Speech for the second year running. But the health secretary, John Reid, said a revised version of the Bill would be submitted to parliament for pre-legislative scrutiny as soon as possible. The mental health minister, Rosie Winterton, added that a code of conduct would be drawn up to set out how the new legislation would work in practice, in a bid to allay fears that it would undermine patients' civil liberties. Although the government has yet to take the Bill forward, the DSPD programme has been extended in high-security prisons and secure hospitals.

© *Guardian Newspapers Limited 2003*

The hidden costs of mental health care

64 per cent spending an average £68 a month

'I do resent paying so much money for something that is essential to my mental health, helps me stay in work and stops me from having another breakdown'
(Survey respondent)

The NHS is failing too many people with mental health problems who go to their GP for help, according to a joint report[1] published today by *Health Which?* and Mind, at the start of Mind Week.[2]

The report – *The Hidden Costs of Mental Health* – reveals too many people having to pay large sums out of their own pockets for care and treatment that helps them cope.

The report is largely based on a survey of people with mental health problems in Mind's networks. It was designed to find out what types of care and treatment people with mental health problems did and didn't get prescribed on the NHS, how much people were paying, and the effect that this was having on their lives.

Astonishingly, almost one in five people who paid for unprescribed care and treatment were forking out more than £100 a month for treatment they felt they needed. And out of the 58 per cent who'd said they had missed out, 70 per cent felt the lack of treatment had hampered their recovery or ability to cope.

Where care or treatment was prescribed by doctors, 45 per cent paid an average £37 a month (mostly for medication, complementary therapies, and counselling/therapy). 51 per cent of people paid an average £61 a month for unprescribed care and treatment (mostly for complementary therapies and counselling/therapy).

Despite a commitment from the Government in its national service framework four years ago to make mental health a priority, this report shows that people with mental health problems are not given equal status

For better mental health

on the NHS and are often forced to foot the bill for their own treatment. The key findings of the report:

- 45 per cent paid an average of just under £40 per month for prescribed care and treatment (often via multiple medications on prescriptions)
- 51 per cent paid around £60 per month for unprescribed care and treatment. 18 per cent of these people paid £100 or more
- 64 per cent had paid or were still paying an average £68 a month for care or treatment (prescribed or not)
- 58 per cent felt they missed out on care or treatment they believed would be helpful. Of these 59 per cent said they could not afford it
- 70 per cent of people who missed out on treatment or paid for it themselves said their recovery was held back or ability to cope reduced.

Kaye McIntosh, Editor, *Health Which?*, said: 'If you break your leg and need physiotherapy you don't have to pay for it. If you have diabetes or epilepsy you don't have to pay for prescriptions. People with chronic mental health problems shouldn't be penalised – especially as financial stress is known to put pressure on our mental wellbeing.'

Richard Brook, Chief Executive of Mind, said: 'The NHS is selling people with mental health problems short. People with enduring mental health problems should not be paying out of their own pockets for essential care and treatment, and it's shocking that over half the people in this survey said they had gone without care or treatment they believe they needed.

'This leaves people with diagnosed mental health problems, who often live on very low incomes, paying huge sums for care that should be available and free of charge on the NHS.'

Mind is calling for free prescriptions for people with mental health problems who need ongoing care and treatment (for medication and non-drug treatments), and for primary care organisations to broaden the range of care and treatment offered to patients.

Mind is using the findings to start a postcard-based petition calling on the Prime Minister to 'ensure that people with mental health problems get the care and treatment they need free of charge'.

References

1 The survey was carried out in 2003 by *Health Which?* and Mind among people with mental health problems who were members of two Mind networks. The report analyses the responses of 455 people who had received care or treatment within the last five years (1,127 questionnaires were sent).

2 Mind and *Health Which?* are released these reports at the start of Mind Week (31st May-7th June 2003) – a week of activity for Mind throughout England and Wales including the launch of a new corporate identity.

■ The above information is reprinted from www.mind.org.uk with permission of Mind (National Association for Mental Health).

Reforming the Mental Health Act

The key issues

In 1998, the Government started on the first substantial reform of mental health legislation for four decades. Their aim was to make law which reflects changes in service delivery over that time, to address perceived public safety concerns, and to bring the law into compliance with the Human Rights Act.

The Richardson Expert Committee was appointed to advise on the content of this new legislation. However, the Government rejected many of the Committee's key recommendations in its own White Paper (2001) and the draft Mental Health Bill (2002). The Government has stated its intention to introduce an amended Mental Health Bill when parliamentary time allows, having now considered the 2000 responses it received to its consultation on the draft Bill.

The Mental Health Alliance

The Mental Health Alliance consists of over 60 organisations from the mental health field. It was established in 2000, following widespread concern about the Government proposals for new mental health legislation. Members of the Alliance include voluntary organisations and service user groups as well as all the professional bodies whose members will be involved in implementing the Mental Health Act. It is an unprecedented alliance of service users, doctors, psychiatrists, nurses, psychologists and lawyers.

What does the Government propose?

Broadly speaking, the Government's proposals are intended to:

- Allow professionals to compulsorily treat mentally ill people in the community as well as in hospital (not allowed under the

Information from the Mental Health Alliance

current Mental Health Act 1983).

- Introduce better safeguards for people who are required to receive compulsory treatment and for informal patients with long-term incapacity.
- Ensure that people with a mental disorder, who are considered at high risk to other people, can more readily be compulsorily treated than under current law.

The Mental Health Alliance's concerns

The Alliance has serious concerns about the draft Mental Health Bill. It disproportionately focuses on perceived dangerousness and risk. It will not achieve the Government's aim of reducing the use of compulsory powers.

We know from our combined experience that a person's health is best served when patients and professionals work together on the basis of mutual respect to bring about an end to a crisis and to promote a recovery. Compulsion can be anti-therapeutic and should be the last resort. We believe that a person should, as far as possible, have control and choice over the treatment that is given to him or her, as is the case for someone with a physical health problem. Discrimination between physical and mental health stigmatises mental health service users.

Improvements in community and inpatient services would better alleviate some of the problems that the Government is seeking to address by the use of compulsory powers. Indeed, the increase in compulsion, which we predict will result from the Bill, may exacerbate problems of public safety by diverting resources from the services that most people with mental health problems need.

The draft Bill would give extensive discretionary powers to, and impose significant duties on, a wide range of professionals. Such powers and duties should be exercised within a strict framework of principles. These need to be stated on the face of the Act.

What the Mental Health Alliance proposes

The Alliance welcomes new legislation, but calls for an Act which provides a legal right to assessment, care and treatment, to help reduce the use of compulsory powers. The following are key principles which should be included in a new Bill:

- Treatment should be the least invasive as well as least restrictive.
- Wherever possible, care and treatment should be provided without recourse to compulsion.
- An obligation on an individual to comply with a care and treatment order should impose a parallel obligation on health and social care authorities to provide appropriate services.
- All powers under the Act should be exercised without discrimination and with respect for individual qualities, abilities and diverse backgrounds.
- Service users should be given all the information necessary to enable them, where possible, to participate in all aspects of their assessment, care, treatment and support.
- Treatment programmes should, as far as possible, reflect the preferences of the service user even when intervention is in the absence of consent.

- For more information see www.mentalhealthalliance.org.uk

© Mental Health Alliance

KEY FACTS

- 1 in 4 people will experience some kind of mental health problem in the course of a year. (p. 1)

- 6 per cent of boys and 16 per cent of girls aged 16-19 are thought to have some form of mental health problem. (p. 1)

- The total cost of mental health problems in England has been estimated at £32 billion. (p. 1)

- Over 91 million working days are lost to mental ill health every year. Half of the days lost through mental illness are due to anxiety and stress conditions. (p. 1)

- People are not born with a mental illness, nor is it part of someone's personality. It is an illness like any other, and can last anything from several weeks to a lifetime. (p. 3)

- Frequent use of recreational drugs can also lead to depression because they may disrupt the brain's chemicals. (p. 6)

- Some people may only ever have one bout of mental illness, which lasts for a few weeks or months. Someone else may have a mental illness all their life, but learn how to live with it with support from friends or through counselling or psychotherapy. (p. 9)

- People who have a mental illness need help from a specialist mental health service (that includes psychiatrists, psychologists, psychotherapists, social workers and nurses who are all highly trained in treating mental illness). (p. 10)

- Alzheimer's disease is the most common form of dementia, affecting around 500,000 people in the UK. (p. 11)

- Much can be done at a practical level to ensure that people with Alzheimer's live as independently as possible for as long as possible. (p. 12)

- A phobia is an irrational fear of an object/situation etc. that would not normally trouble most people. (p. 16)

- People with severe mental illness living in the community are more than twice as likely to be victims of violence as the general public, according to psychiatrists. (p. 18)

- An estimated half a million UK employees believe they are experiencing work-related stress, including anxiety and depression. More than one in ten people is likely to have an anxiety disorder at some stage in their life. (p. 20)

- And yet prejudices abound. A survey in 2000 by the Mental Health Foundation found that 37% of people with mental health problems said they had faced discrimination while looking for work. (p. 22)

- There are many misconceptions about mental health problems, often fuelled by sensationalist media coverage. Research carried out by the Royal College of Psychiatrists in 1998 revealed that 30 per cent of employers interviewed would not, under any circumstances, consider employing people who had experienced mental health problems. (p. 23)

- Mental disorders – like anxiety, depression, eating disorders, drug and alcohol misuse, dementia and schizophrenia – can affect anyone, from any walk of life. In fact, they cause more suffering and disability than any other type of health problem. (p. 25)

- A whole range of different factors – our genetic blueprint, brain chemistry, aspects of our lifestyle, things that have happened to us in the past and our relationships with others – play a part. (p. 25)

- There are many effective treatments for mental disorders. These may include drugs and other physical treatments, talking treatments (psychotherapy) of various kinds, counselling and/or supporting people in their everyday lives in various ways. (p. 25)

- 15% of the UK population will experience a mental illness such as depression, schizophrenia or phobia during their lifetime. (p. 28)

- Currently few children with psychiatric conditions receive treatment. (p. 29)

- In any secondary school of 1,000 pupils there are likely to be: 50 pupils who are seriously depressed; 100 in significant distress; 10-20 pupils with OCD; and 5-10 girls with an eating disorder. (p. 30)

- Every day more than 400 children receive in-depth counselling by ChildLine. (p. 30)

- As many as a third of university students suffer from some form of mental distress, which ranges from clinical disorders to temporary periods of anxiety and depression. About one in 10 undergraduates has one-to-one counselling. (p. 32)

- The World Health Organisation estimates that worldwide up to 20% of children and adolescents have a mental health disorder serious enough to need professional attention. Yet, fewer than one in five received needed treatment. (p. 34)

ADDITIONAL RESOURCES

You might like to contact the following organisations for further information. Due to the increasing cost of postage, many organisations cannot respond to enquiries unless they receive a stamped, addressed envelope.

Alzheimer's Disease International (ADI)
45-46 Lower Marsh
London, SE1 7RG
Tel: 020 7620 3011
Fax: 020 7401 7351
E-mail: info@alz.co.uk
Web site: www.alz.co.uk
ADI is an umbrella organisation of fifty national Alzheimer's Associations around the world.

Alzheimer's Society
Gordon House, 10 Greencoat Place
London, SW1P 1PH
Tel: 020 7306 0606
Fax: 020 7306 0808
E-mail: enquiries@alzheimers.org.uk
Web site: www.alzheimers.org.uk
The UK's leading care and research charity for people with all forms of dementia and their carers.

British Association for Counselling and Psychotherapy (BACP)
35-37 Albert Street
Rugby, Warwickshire, CV21 2SG
Tel: 0870 443 5243
Fax: 0870 443 5161
E-mail: bacp@bacp.co.uk
Web site: www.bacp.co.uk
BACP is an association of over 20,000 practising members, working to promote an understanding of counselling and psychotherapy throughout society.

Mental Health Foundation
7th Floor, 83 Victoria Street
London, SW1H 0HW
Tel: 020 7802 0300
Fax: 020 7802 0301
E-mail: mhf@mhf.org.uk
Web site: www.mentalhealth.org.uk
The leading UK charity working in mental health and learning disabilities.

Mentality
134-138 Borough High Street
London, SE1 1LP
Tel: 020 7716 6777
Fax: 020 7716 6774
E-mail: enquiries@mentality.org.uk
Web site: www.mentality.org.uk

Mentality is the first and only national charity dedicated solely to the promotion of mental health.

Mind
Granta House, 15-19 Broadway
Stratford, London, E15 4BQ
Tel: 020 8519 2122
Fax: 020 8522 1725
E-mail: contact@mind.org.uk
Web site: www.mind.org.uk
Mind works for a better life for everyone with experience of mental distress.

National Phobics Society
Zion Community Resource Centre
339 Stretford Road
Hulme, Manchester, M15 4ZY
Tel: 0161 227 9898
Fax: 0161 227 9862
E-mail: nationalphobic@btconnect.com
Web site: www.phobics-society.org.uk
NPS is a national registered charity formed 30 years ago by a sufferer of agoraphobia for those affected by anxiety disorders.

The National Youth Agency (NYA)
17-23 Albion Street
Leicester, LE1 6GD
Tel: 0116 285 3700
Fax: 0116 285 3777
E-mail: nya@nya.org.uk
Web site: www.nya.org.uk,
www.youthinformation.com
Aims to advance youth work to promote young people's personal and social development, and their voice, influence and place in society.

Royal College of Psychiatrists
17 Belgrave Square
London, SW1X 8PG
Tel: 020 7235 2351
Fax: 020 7235 1935
E-mail: rcpsych@rcpsych.ac.uk
Web site: www.rcpsych.ac.uk
Produces an excellent series of free leaflets on various aspects of mental health. Supplied free of charge but a stamped, addressed envelope is required.

Schizophrenia Association of Great Britain (SAGB)
International Schizophrenia Centre
'Bryn Hyfryd', The Cresent
Bangor, Gwynedd, LL57 2AG
Tel: 01248 354048
Fax: 01248 354048
E-mail: info@sagb.co.uk
Web site: www.sagb.co.uk
Helps and advises people with schizophrenia and their families.

The Scottish Association for Mental Health (SAMH)
Cumbrae House
15 Carlton Court
Glasgow, G5 9JP
Tel: 0141 568 7000
Fax: 0141 568 7001
E-mail: enquire@samh.org.uk
Web site: www.samh.org.uk
SAMH operates a range of services across Scotland for people with mental health problems.

World Federation for Mental Health (WFMH)
PO Box 16810
Alexandria, VA 22302-0810
USA
Tel: + 1 703 838 7543
Fax: + 1 703 519 7648
E-mail: info@wfmh.com
Web site: www.wfmh.com
www.wmhday.net
Promotes among all people and nations, the highest possible level of mental health in its broadest biological, medical, educational, and social aspects.

YoungMinds
102-108 Clerkenwell Road
London, EC1M 5SA
Tel: 020 7336 8445
Fax: 020 7336 8446
E-mail: enquiries@youngminds.org.uk
Web site: www.youngminds.org.uk
YoungMinds is the national charity committed to improving the mental health of all children and young people.

INDEX

ACKNOWLEDGEMENTS

The publisher is grateful for permission to reproduce the following material.

While every care has been taken to trace and acknowledge copyright, the publisher tenders its apology for any accidental infringement or where copyright has proved untraceable. The publisher would be pleased to come to a suitable arrangement in any such case with the rightful owner.

Chapter One: What is Mental Illness?

Statistics on mental health, © Mental Health Foundation, *What are mental health problems?*, © The Scottish Association for Mental Health (SAMH), *The lowdown on mental breakdowns*, © 2004 NetDoctor.co.uk – HMG Worldwide 2003, *Young people with mental health problems*, © Mental Health Foundation, *Depression*, © The Daily Mail, 2003, *Virtually anyone can become mentally ill*, © Crown copyright is reproduced with the permission of Her Majesty's Stationery Office, *Mental illness in your family?*, © YoungMinds 2003, *Alzheimer's disease*, © Alzheimer's Society, *About dementia*, © Alzheimer's Disease International (ADI), *A beginner's article about schizophrenia*, © Schizophrenia Association of Great Britain (SAGB), *Mental illness is an illness like any other*, © Crown copyright is reproduced with the permission of Her Majesty's Stationery Office, *Anxiety disorders*, © The National Phobics Society, *Neurotic disorders*, © Crown copyright is reproduced with the permission of Her Majesty's Stationery Office, *Mental illness and violence*, © Guardian Newspapers Limited 2003, *Mental illness – dispelling the stigma*, © Everywoman Ltd, *Attitudes towards mental illness*, © Crown copyright is reproduced with the permission of Her Majesty's Stationery Office, *The Bruno effect*,

© Guardian Newspapers Limited 2003, *Mental illness* © Mental Health Foundation, *Mental health in the workplace*, © mentality.

Chapter Two: Seeking Help

Emotional health and wellbeing, © Crown copyright is reproduced with the permission of Her Majesty's Stationery Office, *Mental disorders*, © 2004 Royal College of Psychiatrists, *Descriptions of mentally ill people*, © Crown copyright is reproduced with the permission of Her Majesty's Stationery Office, *Positive steps to mental health*, © mentality, *About mental illness*, © National Youth Agency, *Treatment of children and teenagers*, © Mental Health Care, *Mental health in education*, © British Association for Counselling and Psychotherapy (BACP), *The saddest university challenge of all*, © Telegraph Group Limited, London 2004, *Student mental health reminder*, © Mental Health Foundation, *Improved services for young people*, © World Federation for Mental Health (WFMH), *Anti-depressant drugs*, © Crown copyright is reproduced with the permission of Her Majesty's Stationery Office, *How to beat depression*, © The Daily Mail, 2004, *Mental Health Bill – questions and answers*, © Guardian Newspapers Limited 2003, *The hidden costs of mental health care*, © 2003 Mind (National Association for Mental Health), *Reforming the Mental Health Act*, © Mental Health Alliance.

Photographs and illustrations:

Pages 1, 13, 28, 37: Simon Kneebone; pages 3, 10: Pumpkin House; pages 8, 15, 29: Bev Aisbett; page 18: Angelo Madrid; page 21: Don Hatcher.

Craig Donnellan
Cambridge
April, 2004